Parenting Together Apart: For the Residential Parent

Parenting Together Apart: For the Residential Parent

Working Together for Your Child's Best Interest

Brette Sember, JD

Copyright © 2019 by Brette McWhorter Sember

ISBN 978-0-9995942-4-7

All rights reserved. No part of this book may be reproduced in any form or by any electronic or mechanical means including information storage and retrieval systems-except in the case of brief quotations embodied in critical articles or reviews, or in the case of the exercises in this book solely for the personal use of the purchaser without permission in writing from its publisher, Sember Resources. Some content in this book was previously published under the titles *The Visitation Handbook* and *How to Parent With Your Ex*

Published by: Sember Resources

This publication is designed to provide accurate and authoritative information in regard to the subject matter covered. It is sold with the understanding that the publisher is not engaged in rendering legal, accounting, or other professional service. If legal advice or other expert assistance is required, the services of a competent professional person should be sought.

From a Declaration of Principles Jointly Adopted by a Committee of the American Bar Association and a Committee of Publishers and Associations

This product is not a substitute for legal advice.
Disclaimer required by Texas statutes.

I would like to thank the children I worked with when I was practicing law, who led me to the deeply personal insights behind this book. Having worked so closely with them and having been so involved in their lives, I felt deeply compelled to write a book that would help their parents improve their situations. I offer my deepest respect and admiration for the judges and court personnel who handle these cases with such care and empathy.

Table of Contents

PREFACE xiii

INTRODUCTION 1
  What This Book Will Do 1
  Avoid the Revolving Door 2
  Help for All You're Going Through 2
  How to Use This Book 3
  What This Book Cannot Do 4

CHAPTER 1   FACING REALITY 6
  Understanding Terms 6
    Joint Custody with Visitation 7
    Sole Custody and Visitation 7
    Shared Custody 7
  Do Not Get Hung Up on Words 8
  Things Will Not Be the Same 9
  Look at the Other Side 9
  Let Go of Anger and Blame 11
  Dealing with Loss 13
  Respect the Other Parent's Time 13
  Changing the Schedule 14

Contents

CHAPTER 2   **YOUR CHANGING RELATIONSHIP WITH YOUR CHILD** **17**
    The Effects of Divorce 18
    Reactions by Ages 18
    Gender Differences 19
    Riding the Ups and Downs 19
    Dealing with the Bad Times 20
    Anger and Resentment 22
    Finding Out What Your Child Thinks 23
    Do Not Say Anything Bad about the Other Parent 23
    Social Media 24
    When Your Child Blames You 24
    Dealing with the Fear of Abandonment 25
    Dealing with Divided Loyalties 27
    Dealing with Your Changing Feelings 27
    Dealing with Your Child's Changing Feelings 29
    Be Patient 29

CHAPTER 3   **COMMUNICATING WITH YOUR CHILD** **31**
    What to Say to Your Child 32
    Things You Should Not Say 34
    Listening to Your Child 37

CHAPTER 4   **RULES FOR YOUR CHILD** **39**
    To Parents with Sole Custody 40
    Whose Rules: Yours or the Other Parent's 41
    Creating Rules Together 42
    Discussing Rules with Your Child 43
    Creating Your Own Rules 46
    The Other Parent's Rules 47
    Rules That Are Wrong 47
    Misinformation 48
    Bending the Rules 48

Contents

	Changing Rules for Your Changing Child	48
	When Rules Are Broken	49
	Final Thoughts about Rules	49
CHAPTER 5	**RULES FOR YOURSELF**	**51**
	Deal with Your Emotions	51
	Work with the Other Parent	52
	Do Not Speak Negatively about the Other Parent	53
	Talk to Your Child	54
	Respect Parenting Time	55
	Avoid Confrontations	55
	Talk Honestly, But Carefully about the Divorce	55
	Make Real Promises to Your Child	56
	Decide Who You Are	56
	Be on Time	57
	Be Present	57
	Make the Best of It	57
CHAPTER 6	**COMMUNICATING WITH THE OTHER PARENT**	**60**
	Try to Develop a New Relationship	60
	Set Co-Parenting Rules for Yourselves	61
	Be Flexible	63
	Develop a Written Schedule Together	63
	Bite Your Tongue	64
	Divide Responsibilities	64
	Arguments	65
	Setting Up Times to Talk	65
	Getting Help	66
	When All Else Fails: Try the Business Transaction Approach	66
	When It is Unbearable	67

Contents

CHAPTER 7   **ENCOURAGING AND ASSISTING WITH VISITATION** **70**
     Your Feelings about Time with the Other Parent 71
     Your Responsibility for Parenting Time 72
     Kids Who Don't Want to Go 73
     When Your Child Would Rather Be There 75
     Dealing with Transitions 76
     When the Other Parent Is a Crappy Parent 78
     Helping Your Child with Long-Distance
         Parenting 79
     Vacations 80
     Coping with All that Stuff 80
     Medication 83

CHAPTER 8   **DEALING WITH SCHEDULES** **84**
     The Schedule 84
     Understanding Your Child's Schedule 86
     Dealing with Conflicts 87
     When to Say No 88
     Your Child's Friends 88
     Changing Your Schedule 88
     Equal Time Problems 89
     Solving Confusion about Schedules 90
     Dealing with Schedule Violations 92

CHAPTER 9   **HOLIDAYS** **94**
     Being Realistic 94
     Holidays with Your Child 95
     Holidays without Your Child 96
     Sharing Holidays 99
     Gifts 99
     Birthdays 100
     Solving Holiday Problems 101

Contents

CHAPTER 10 THE SINGLE PARENT LIFE **102**
    Coping with the Changes 102
    Running a House Alone 103
    Making Decisions 104
    Creating a New Routine 104
    Having a Life 104
    Scheduling 105
    Parenting Alone 105
    You Do Not Have to Do This Alone 106

CHAPTER 11 DEALING WITH OTHER PEOPLE **108**
    Schools 108
    Health Care Workers 110
    Your Family and Friends 112
    The Other Parent's Family and Friends 112
    Your New Partner 113
    Stepfamilies 115
    The Other Parent's New Partner 115

CHAPTER 12 SPECIAL SITUATIONS **119**
    Physical or Sexual Abuse 119
    Substance Abuse 120
    Mental Illness 120
    Violation of the Terms of the Custody Order . 122
    Bad Parenting by the Other Parent 122
    Nonpayment of Child Support 123
    Changing Custody 124
    You Want to End Visitation 125
    Supervised Visitation 126
    Gender and Sexuality 127
    Teens 128
    Parents Who Refuse to Exercise Visitation .. 128
    Things that Supercede Visitation 129

Contents

                A Sick Child · 130
                Relocation · 131
                Special Needs Children · 131
                Food Allergies · 132
                Parental Abduction · 132
                Military Personnel/Travel for Work · · · · · · · · · · · · · · 133
                Imprisonment · 133
                Stay at Home Parents · 134
                Homeschooling · 135
                If Your Child Is Adopted · 135
                Grandparent Visitation · 135
                Shared Parenting · 136
                Shared Residence · 137

CHAPTER 13 CHILDREN'S AGES AND STAGES · · · · · · · · · · · 139
                Infants · 139
                Toddlers · 142
                Preschoolers · 143
                Elementary Children · 143
                Preteens · 144
                Teens · 145
                Adult Children · 147
                Siblings · 147

                CONCLUSION · 149

APPENDIX A SAMPLE PARENTING PLANS · · · · · · · · · · · · · · · 151

APPENDIX B RESOURCES · 155

                ABOUT THE AUTHOR · 167

Preface

Many books offer psychological perspectives on co-parenting, single parenthood, and life after divorce. This isn't one of those books. Written by a divorce and family attorney, this book gives you a practical roadmap for living with a co-parenting plan. The author worked in family court, representing both children and parents. She saw the problems families face as they try to navigate through visitation and the changes it brings. This book is filled with practical tips that are based on her experience with real families.

There are lots of books that tell you how to get yourself and your child through the actual divorce or split, but none tell you how you are going to live in this new situation. This book is your complete guide to dealing with parenting after divorce. It is difficult to adjust to a completely new life, and it is difficult to continue to manage visitation and parenting through the years following a divorce or separation. Living with this new plan is like nothing else you have done before. Many families have trouble coping with the challenges post – divorce and post-separation parenting brings. They end up returning to court, where they let the court work out their disputes and make changes to their schedule. Some families end up in a revolving door syndrome, where they are constantly returning to court. This constant

Preface

uncertainty takes its toll on the parents – and especially on the child. Whether you have sole custody or joint custody, you are still both parents together and your child will benefit if you can learn to co-parent together effectively.

This book will help you avoid the revolving door. It is a guide for you to use now, and for you to return to again and again as your child grows, your situation changes, and new challenges and obstacles arise. Your co-parenting situation will always be in flux, so learning how to prepare for and work through the changes thrown your way is an important part of parenting together.

It is important to note that both males and females take on both of the parenting roles discussed in this book. If you are a nonresidential mother or a residential father, or if you are same sex parents, you might sometimes feel like you are in an unusual role. This book helps all divorced and separated parents, regardless of their gender and regardless of which role they are in.

The book carefully refers to "the other parent" throughout the text. This is a purposeful attempt to get you to think of him or her in this way. He or she is your child's other parent, and it is important for your child's health and well-being that you respect and accept this fact. For the most part to avoid thinking of him or her as your ex, former spouse, (or other choice names) and so on. Keep your focus on your joint parenting responsibilities.

This wording is also used because many parents never marry each other. This book is written for you whether you have been married or not, are divorced or separated, are currently in the midst of divorcing or separating, or even if you and the other parent never even had any long-term relationship at all, but did have a child together.

The book generally refers to "your child" or "your kid." Obviously, many people have more than one child. If you have more than one child, apply the advice given to all of your children. When the text refers to your child this generally includes children and teens of all ages. If a situation is different for teens or another age group, it will be specifically mentioned. The book will help you understand the different reactions children will have at different ages and also discusses how sibling relationships are affected by visitation.

Both parents are needed in a child's life. You should be commended for wanting to focus on your child's needs. This book will help you through the

Preface

difficulties parenting apart brings, and will help you and your child make the most of your situation.

Refer to this book when you are first adjusting to parenting apart and in the future. Problems and concerns that you cannot anticipate are certain to come up at a later time. Keep this book as a reference guide to use for those future situations down the road.

Note

If your relationship with the other parent was abusive, or if you feel that you could be in danger because of the other parent, this book is not designed for you. If you feel you are in danger, speak to your attorney or get help from a shelter for battered spouses. If you feel your child is in danger from the other parent, contact your attorney and your local department of family and children's services.

Introduction

You have faced the end of your marriage or relationship, been through the courts or mediation to obtain a parenting plan, and now your child is living more than 50% of the time with you and spending time with the other parent. You may not consider your parenting arrangement to be ideal but it's something you need to learn to live with. Now that you are through the craziness of the legal process and the difficult emotions that accompany it, your first order of business has to be taking everything that has happened in your life, in court, and inside you, and just let it settle in. Getting through it is a huge relief. But there's more work ahead.

What This Book Will Do

There are many books and resources available to help you heal the pain of divorce. This is not one of them. This book is designed to help you manage, understand, and maximize your parenting time and help you learn to work effectively with the other parent. The book is written not by a psychologist or social worker, but by an attorney who has spent much time in court and in the homes of families facing and working through parenting issues. The author worked one-on-one with parents and children, many of them on a daily basis, as they struggled through the unraveling and reformation of their families. Some families were able to make their new situation work for them, but many more could not. These were the families who returned to court again and again as one or both of the parents continued to have problems living with the new arrangement.

Avoid the Revolving Door

Many families get caught in a revolving door, returning every few months to court to try once again to get something changed, when what really needs to change is their behavior and attitudes. This book offers practical, to-the-point solutions for the problems that you as a residential parent are facing or about to face. If you can follow the advice in this book, you can avoid the family court revolving door syndrome and reduce conflict with the other parent.

The book is designed to help you through the confusing, upsetting, and sometimes hurtful process of being the parent who primarily resides with your child. No matter what has led you to this point, you are your child's parent, and the role you play in his or her life is incredibly important. Your child has two parents and needs to be part of both your lives.

Help for All You're Going Through

You may feel constrained by the schedule you have to follow; you may find that it isn't completely convenient for you, and you probably feel that it is not entirely fair. You may also have reservations about the other parent's abilities or behavior. Despite all of that, it is up to you to help your child cope with the new arrangement, as well as find a way for you to live with it. As the parent who spends the most time with your child, it is up to you to set the tone for how the new arrangement will be handled. You are responsible for making sure that the time you have with your child is the best it can be and that your child gets the benefits of time with the other parent. This book contains pointers and tips to help you make the most of what you have and to help your child cope with the schedule and continue to love and have a good relationship with the other parent. It is based on the author's experiences working with families that have gone through the same process you are now going through.

This book will discuss what you can expect from your child, yourself, and the other parent, as well as other people in your life and your child's life with regard to the parenting schedule. The book focuses on how to manage the schedule as a practical matter, how to cope with it on an emotional level, how to help your child cope with it, and how to use it to benefit both of you.

Each chapter deals with specific problems that come up and addresses the different problems that come with children of different ages. The advice is based on the author's firsthand, up close experiences as a divorce and family attorney and mediator. The author's years of experience working as a Law Guardian for children who are the subjects of custody and visitation cases brings the powerful and unique perspective of one who has watched the divorce process through the eyes of those children.

Many parents walk out of the courthouse with an order giving them residential custody and visitation to the other parent, and feel that they have won. You might also have walked out of the courthouse feeling you got most of what you wanted but that the other parent scored some victories as well, meaning that the road ahead can be challenging. The thing to remember is there are no winners and no victories. There is only the road ahead. You have to accept that whatever the judge decided or you agreed to is now how you will live your life. You must focus on helping your child deal with the arrangement and on making the arrangement as easy to live with as possible for both of you. This book will help you do just that.

How to Use This Book

Read this book and pay careful attention to the chapters that speak to your immediate concerns or problems. Keep the book handy and consult it as you experience new problems and different stages.

The book is designed to be your guide through the maze of being the residential parent and coping with joint parenting. Many parents resolve their custody cases through settlement or a trial, head out to live with their parenting plan, and end up back in the courtroom within a year because of practical problems with visitation. These problems can stem from any of the parties – the nonresidential parent, you, or even the child. Problems can include things such as a child not wanting to go to the other parent, a residential parent who tries to avoid visitation, and even disagreements over things like the child's laundry or homework. Divorce or separation completely rearranges the lives of everyone involved. An adjustment period is necessary. Many families do not make it through the adjustment period without having to seek legal intervention. This book will help you with that difficult period and will steer you away from the pitfalls that bring so many families back through the courtroom door.

There is a companion book to this one called Parenting Together Apart: For the Nonresidential Parent. It can be helpful for you to read this other book to get an idea of what the other parent is dealing with. It's also a great idea for the other parent to read the companion book, so that you can both be on the same page.

What This Book Cannot Do

What this book cannot do is change the facts of your situation. If you are certain that the parenting plan you have is not in the best interest of your child or is completely incompatible with your schedule, you need to contact an attorney or deal with the issue in mediation. Should you ever become concerned that your child is being physically or mentally abused, you need to take immediate action and contact your local police department or child protection agency. This book also cannot change the other parent. However, this book can help you learn to work with him or her.

Your parenting plan or custody and visitation order is nothing more than a schedule that organizes everyone's time. It is not a decree that one of you is a bad or unimportant parent and that the other one is the better parent or has more clout with regard to the child. It is merely a time management tool.

Parenting Together Apart: For the Residential Parent

Learning how to make the most of what you have will help your child be healthy and feel loved – and will bring you sanity. You can make time with the other parent a wonderful part of your child's life while maintaining an equally wonderful relationship with your child. Making the best of this situation is the best thing you will ever do for your child.

Chapter 1

Facing Reality

Now that the dust has cleared and you know what kind of parenting arrangement you are going to be living with, it's time to face reality. First, you need to completely understand your parenting plan details and what rights you have.

Next, you will need to take a look at what that really means for you and your child. While it may be hard to adjust to your new life, you will find that there are many bright spots in it. This chapter will help you get a grip on your life and help you see what you have to smile about.

Understanding Terms

Now that you have residential, primary, or legal custody, you might not be entirely sure what rights that gives you. First, you need to read the judge's order or your settlement agreement carefully. The following are some of the possible custody and visitation arrangements you might have (which might be called a parenting plan, custody order, co-parenting plan, shared time agreement, parenting access plan, or other terms).

Parenting Together Apart: For the Residential Parent

Joint Custody with Visitation
You and the other parent share joint legal custody, with the child residing with you and visiting with the other parent. Your order might call you "joint custodians." Joint custody means you are supposed to make decisions together about the child, such as where he or she goes to school, whether to have medical procedures done, etc. Joint custodians are expected to be able to communicate with each other. You, as the person the child spends more than half the time with, have residential custody. The other parent has visitation or parenting time according to a schedule or when you both agree to it.

Sole Custody and Visitation
In this arrangement, you have sole legal custody and the other parent has visitation. This means the child lives primarily with you, and that you make most of the decisions about the child and are not required to get the other parent's input. The other parent has visitation at set times or at times as agreed upon.

Shared Custody
In this scenario, the child splits his or her time equally between you and the other parent. Both of you are responsible for making decisions about the child. Neither is considered to be the residential parent.

If you are not sure which type of arrangement you have, call your attorney or mediator for help in understanding the wording in your judgment or order. The most important thing to remember about the different arrangements is that they are just words. Your child is still your child. Your child is still the other parent's child as well. Even though you now have specific times with your child, you still need to parent together. Learn the legal term and then forget it. Your focus should be on your relationship with your child and on cooperating with the other parent, not on a phrase and how it makes you feel; how it makes the other parent feel; or, how other people react to it.

Do Not Get Hung Up on Words

You should not get hung up on the words custody and visitation. You also should not become too focused on the word "co-parenting." These are simply terms we use to describe the situation that exists after divorce. When you and the other parent lived in the same house, you were parents together, period. One of you may have spent more time with your child. Today you're still parents and one of you may spend more time with your child. The only thing that has changed is that you are not doing this under the same roof. It is important that you both continue to be parents and that your child continues to see you both as his or her parents.

Children are not something you get custody of. The only time people are taken into custody is when they are arrested. You are parenting together. There is nothing remotely militant about being a parent. Parents do not visit with their children. Parents live with their children. This is what you will both now be doing, except you will be doing it in different homes and at different times. In fact, many attorneys, mediators, and judges are moving away from this poor choice of words and are now talking about parenting time, parenting access, parenting plans, and parenting schedules. Try using these words because they will make your child feel more comfortable and will also make the other parent feel more comfortable. Try to see past the words to what is at the heart of the matter – your child. The other parent is much more than a visitor to your child.

NONTRADITIONAL FAMILIES

It's important to note that no two families are the same and today's families facing divorce and separation include same-sex and adoptive families as well as those created with assisted reproductive technology. Courts do not care how someone got to be a parent. Whether a parent carried a child, contributed genetic material, entered into surrogacy, or signed adoption papers, that parent is as much of a parent as any other. The courts don't consider the path to parenthood and it's important that you and the other parent don't either. If you are a biological parent and

> the other parent is not, there can be a tendency to feel as if you are more entitled to parenting time. The thing to remember is your child is equally emotionally connected to both of you as parents, no matter what the genetics of the situation are.

Things Will Not Be the Same

Now that you have digested the legal terms and gotten past them, you need to face another mental challenge. Nothing in your life will ever be the same. That statement may seem to be huge, unfair, and unbearable, but it is true. Your own relationship with your child's other parent did not work and you have parted. You are living apart, and this means that in order for your child to receive the benefit of being loved and supported by both parents, all three of you now must make changes and concessions to adapt to this new way of life.

Just because a situation is different, it does not mean it cannot be as good—or better—than the previous situation. Think about how unhappy everyone was when the relationship was coming apart. It was not a healthy situation for your child or for anyone else—which is why you got out. You now have the chance to build your own life, find happiness, and make your own way without the burdens of that relationship. Part of the price of freedom is that you will have to make arrangements in order to include your child in your life and make sure the other parent is included in your child's life. This means that you will have to make some concessions. The situation will not always meet your ideal. However, it will be the family your child has, and your job is to make the best of it and focus on the positives.

Look at the Other Side

Just because your child will be spending more time with you does not make you the parenting god, so to speak. It is very important that you recognize that both parents are important to your child and to a well-rounded parenting arrangement. You cannot change the other parent and you also shouldn't try to control what happens at his or her house. You cannot change his or her behavior. And, you cannot (and should not try to) stop your child from loving him or her. Accept that your child has two parents who are equally important in his or her life. Your child has—and needs to continue to have—two parents who can, on some level, work together as parents. You may have divorced or separated from the other parent, but for the rest of your lives you will be parents together. Even when you're old and gray, you will still share this child and this family. The path to happiness is to find a way to make it work. It will never be perfect, but it can be functional.

Take a step back and view the situation from the other parent's point of view. He or she might feel stripped of his or her parenting rights. Being told you aren't good enough or don't measure up is horrible. A judge or an agreement has essentially pushed him or her aside and given you more time with your child. Having someone say you don't deserve more time with your kid hurts. He or she feels afraid, cheated, and lost, whether or not you believe he or she has a right to feel this way. The other parent might feel you are to blame for what's happened. Many times nonresidential parents react to this situation by being mean, hurtful, or by withdrawing. Internal pain is often a reason to strike out at others. Think about how you would feel if you were to switch positions. You might feel the same way.

Whether you believe the parenting plan is right or not, your child needs to continue to have a relationship with the other parent. Your job is to make sure that happens. This is part of the responsibility of being the residential parent. You must push aside the negative feelings you have about the other parent. In order for your child to grow up feeling loved, healthy, and secure, it's your responsibility to make room in your child's life for the other parent.

You might be wondering, Why am I responsible for his or her relationship with my child? You're not responsible for it, but you should support it since this is what is best for your child. You love your child so much that you want to give him or her the world. A healthy, ongoing relationship with the other parent is truly what your child needs. You should try to make sure that your child continues to be close to you, but that there is also a closeness with the other parent. Your relationship with—and resentment, anger, hurt, and tangled emotions towards—the other parent must remain separate from this.

Let Go of Anger and Blame

You and the other parent broke up because you fought, were unhappy, hurt each other, disappointed each other, or blamed each other for things. Thankfully, that scenario is over. You don't need to live with anger on a daily basis now. You are certainly going to continue to feel some anger, and you probably have many things to blame the other parent for but it doesn't need to be a central part of your life now. Work on letting go of what happened in your relationship.

If you continue to focus on your anger and blame (no matter how well-justified it may be), you're never going to be able to get past it and parent together without conflict. There is no way you can always be angry without having it affect your child. As difficult as the divorce or separation has been for you, it has been at least a hundred times more difficult for your child.

Everything that's happened has been magnified in your child's eyes, increased by total or partial incomprehension, and heavily laced with emotional insecurity and fear. When you are angry around your child, he or she unconsciously interprets some or all of that anger as being directed towards him or her. Think about this: every time you are angry, your child assumes it is because of him or her. Your anger has a very strong effect.

To have successful relationships with your child and the other parent, you should try to focus mentally and emotionally. Anger is going to get in the way. You need some space in your head and your heart to make a plan for how you are going to parent from now on. If you are angry, you are using a lot of energy and effort for your anger. There's never a lot of room for clear thinking when anger is so consuming. Everything you feel is justified. Everything you feel is normal. But at the same time, it is probably not particularly helpful.

Remind yourself that the other parent is not worth all the effort and angst. None of this means that you are not going to experience anger in the future. It is most assured that you and the other parent will continue to push each other's buttons. The two of you had a lot of practice and it has become a habit. You're going to have to steer through these situations in the months and years ahead. If you haul along baggage from the past, it is just going to be harder to manage. You are also experiencing a lot of hurt and loss. Some things have happened that you did not deserve. You may have been rejected or insulted. Take the time to grieve for what you have lost, to feel the pain that is associated with a relationship ending, and then face the future. You may never completely get over what has happened and in a way, that pain will always be a part of you. But it's time to step forward and start a new parenting relationship that is free of that baggage.

TIPS FOR MOVING FORWARD
- Decide that the past is the past. It's over. Walk away from it
- Let yourself go through the natural grieving process associated with divorce or separation. It's okay to be sad, angry, and hurt.
- Let go of your anger. It is not helping you.
- Think about your future and make plans for what you want and what you will do.
- Take it slow. A fresh start is a gradual process. Give yourself time.
- Focus on the love you have for your child. That is what really matters.
- Look at things positively. Think about the time you have with your child. It's a wonderful gift to have dedicated time with your child without the other parent involved.
- Make your child the center of your world instead of your problems with the other parent.
- You're not perfect and you're going to make mistakes. It's normal.

You aren't perfect and, of course, you're going to slip up. Try very hard to focus on your child and not on your past relationship with the other parent. You have a lot of work ahead, but you can get through this.

Parenting Together Apart: For the Residential Parent

Dealing with Loss

When the divorce or custody case was initially decided or settled, you might have felt in some ways like you were the winner because of how the parenting plan ended up. After all you now have more time to spend with your child than the other parent. As you move forward though, you might also start to feel as if you have lost something. You don't get to spend every day with your child and there are moments in his or her life you will not be present for. You most likely won't be with your child for all holidays. You may never have been away for your child for more than an overnight and now the other parent might have a whole with your child sometimes. Some residential parents feel a deep sense of loss for this reason, particularly those who were stay-at-home parents before the divorce.

Your child will now be away from you for periods of time, while you used to see each other every day. You probably resent the other parent for taking time away from you. You need to realize that although you will not have as much time with your child as you did before, you still have more time than the other parent, and you should try not begrudge him or her the time that is allotted. Keep in mind that your loss is your child's gain. He or she needs to have time with the other parent. The time you have with your child is your time alone, without any interference from the other parent. Enjoy what you have and know that the time your child spends with the other parent is important.

Respect the Other Parent's Time

One of this book's main messages is to focus on your child. Your first thought may be that you have been doing exactly that, and it is part of the reason you needed to end the relationship and have your child live with you. Don't lose sight of that and continue to focus on your child, but remember that you absolutely must allow the other parent to continue to have an important and meaningful role in your child's life. You are probably relieved not to have to spend time with the other parent, but your child certainly does not feel that way. Make sure you respect the other parent's time with your child and role in your child's life, and don't put up roadblocks.

This also means that you should try to have a positive and encouraging attitude about the other parent's role. Convey to your child that you want him or her to spend time with the other parent. Demonstrate that you respect this new, separate relationship your child has with the other parent. Don't convey feelings of resentment or anger about the other parent's presence and involvement in your child's life, even if you have them.

Focusing on your child also means that you should reevaluate your entire situation. When you see your ex, you may see red, but turn your eyes to your child and make him or her the focus of the situation. When you fail to respect or allow time with the other parent, you are not punishing the other parent: you are punishing your child. It is also important that you make time to spend with your child. It is easy for this to get lost in the craziness of everyday life. Make a point to spend real, one-on-one time with your child on a regular basis and give him or her your full attention.

As you experience being a residential parent, it will be difficult at first to juggle all the changes you are facing. You feel afraid, overwhelmed by being alone, lost, scared, and abandoned. Scheduled time with the other parent may feel like a disruption or an intrusion. The good news is that it will get easier and you will find a new routine that incorporates the parenting schedule as a part of normal life. Your child will come to adjust to it as well, and you will become comfortable with your new family routine.

Changing the Schedule

If you have sole custody, or you share joint custody with the other parent with residential custody, your child will have your home as his or her home base or residence. The other parent will see your child at the times outlined in your court order or judgment. What many parents do not realize is that you are not required to stick to the schedule set in the order or judgment. You and the other parent can agree to arrange visitation at any other times, change the times that are scheduled by the court, have the child spend more or less time with the other parent or basically make any adjustments you want to. <u>However, you must both agree to any change.</u> You must be certain that you can trust the other parent to stick to the changes you agree to, or you need to get it in writing so that you have proof of the agreement in case there is ever a problem.

It is true that a court order is a legal, binding document. However, almost all custody or divorce decrees add that in addition to the scheduled visitation times, the parents shall have time with the child "as agreed upon." This gives you the freedom to change the schedule as needed. Judges want parents to take control of their schedule and adjust it to suit their family's needs. They do not want families returning to court to change pick-up times or arrange for a change to the holiday schedule. There are simply not enough resources for judges to be able to mediate every small alteration to every family's parenting plan. The court wants the two of you to become self-sufficient and learn to work together to make changes. If you make big long-lasting changes to the plan, you should get those changes incorporated into an updated order or agreement so it is in writing, but in general if you want to switch weekends, juggle things so the other parent has an extra afternoon per week, or rearrange the holiday schedule, you should go ahead as long as you both agree and are completely clear about the change.

A parenting plan is not something that is set in stone. It should be something that changes as the child and parents change. What works for a one-year-old will not work when the child is in kindergarten or in high school. You and the other parent should view the parenting plan or visitation schedule as a guideline, not as a hard and set law. (See Chapter 6 for more about communicating with the other parent.)

WAYS TO FOCUS ON YOUR CHILD
- Think about the time you have, not the time you are missing.
- Don't let your child see or feel the anger you have towards the other parent.
- Make time with the other parent a priority because it's important for your child.
- Encourage and support the scheduled times between your child and the other parent.

- Show respect for your child's relationship with the other parent.
- Encourage your child to have contact with the other parent when they are apart.
- Consider how your child is feeling and think about how you can help.
- Arrange to spend one-on-one time with your child when you can give him or her your undivided attention.
- Remember that you are not any less of a parent simply because you are sharing your child's time.

Chapter 2

Your Changing Relationship with Your Child

If you haven't realized it yet, your relationship with your child changes as a result of the divorce or separation. Your child probably grew up being parented by two parents. You and the other parent made decisions together, or at least you were both involved in some way. Now your child is parented by two parents who are in separate homes and have little input from each other. Your child has gone from getting a kind of average of the two of you to getting the two extremes. This is a huge change for everyone.

Your child is dealing with one or possibly two new residences, as well as a schedule that could be very confusing and hard to adjust to. All of these changes have had an effect on your child and may cause him or her to act differently. You are learning to be a single parent, with no backup from the other parent. You will find that this will cause you to act differently too.

You've probably gone through some rough times. The breakup of a relationship, a court proceeding, and all the deep emotional difficulties with all of this has been very stressful. You're probably not who you used to be. You can see that both you and your child have changed, so it makes sense that your relationship has changed and will continue to change.

The Effects of Divorce

A great deal of research has been conducted to study the effects of divorce on children. While these studies reveal some basic truths, the fact is that each child is unique and may react differently from other children. Read about some of the common effects, but keep in mind that your child may not be typical and that not every child experiences most or all of these reactions. Be aware of what to look for so you can step in if you need to.

CHILDREN'S COMMON REACTIONS TO DIVORCE
- Sadness and grief
- Anger
- Desire to place blame (on parents and on themselves)
- Fear of abandonment and loss
- Divided loyalties (wanting to be loyal to both parents, even when this is impossible)
- Denial
- School and social problems
- Withdrawal
- Low self-esteem
- Inability to trust people or form bonds
- Physical symptoms, such as stomachaches and headaches

Reactions by Ages

Expect preschool children to blame themselves and possibly to regress or go backwards a bit in their development. School-age children experience worries about the future and are at a higher risk of depression. These children also often act out. Teenagers frequently take sides in a divorce and experience financial worries because of it. They also feel negatively about marriage as an institution and try to physically and emotionally distance themselves from home and home life. Teens will likely engage in social media as they work through the situation, expressing emotions there. (See Chapter 13 for more information about how reactions differ by age.)

Gender Differences

Girls with heterosexual parents are likely to react by trying to make connections with males or by trying to bring male influences into the mother's home. Girls, in general, try to be perfect to prevent future problems. They want to fix it and think that if they can start by being perfect themselves it will heal the relationship. Boys with heterosexual parents are likely to react by trying to fill their father's shoes by acting as the man of the house at the mother's home. Boys may try to suppress their feelings of great sadness and may become more aggressive as the suppressed feeling need a way to come out. Low self esteem can be a problem for both genders. Kids of divorce are more likely to lose their virginity earlier than other teens. (For more information about children's reactions, refer to the resources listed in Appendix B.)

Riding the Ups and Downs

One of the most important things to expect about the adjustment you and your child are making is that there will be ups and downs. You may have a terrific week together and feel as if you are getting back on track, followed by a few bad weeks. Remember that adjusting to the situation is a lengthy process. Nothing that happens is going to be set in stone—good times and bad times are to be expected. Everything is going to be in flux for quite a while.

When you are experiencing good times, enjoy them. Let yourself relax and be happy. Your child might return from the other parent's home without you having a fight with the other parent or your child might be thrilled to see you. You might spend some time together and find yourselves being comfortable and feeling really connected. If you have a day like this, soak it up.

Be realistic though and don't expect it to last forever. If your child has a tantrum and says, "I hate you," tells you he or she would rather live with the other parent, or complains that you don't do things the same way as the other parent, don't see it as the end of the world. All children have short attention spans, all children have tantrums, and no parent is perfect. Don't expect perfection from yourself or your child and you will not be disappointed. Try to remember that as a parent, it is not your job to make sure your child is happy every moment and has everything he or she wants. It is your job to make and enforce rules, give and receive love openly, and be willing to communicate. (Read Chapter 4 for more about establishing rules.)

Try to see everything that happens as part of the big picture. One bad day does not seem so terrible in the context of a month or a year. Keep your perspective and remember that no matter what happens, it is not the end of the world.

You also need to understand that even as you and your child become accustomed to the new arrangement, changes will happen in your lives that can send things up into the air again. You might meet someone new that you care about, or your teen might get a job or your elementary age child might start playing on a sports team. You and your child are always changing, and your times together will be constantly changing as well.

Dealing with the Bad Times

Just as you can't have good times all the time, neither can you have bad times that never end. You may have some very difficult periods of time to get through, but they will pass. The beauty of children is that they are always growing and changing.

If you find that there are truly no happy times, you need to evaluate your situation. Are you the one who is perceiving everything as unhappy? If so, you might want to talk to a mental health professional. You have been through a lot and there is nothing wrong with finding someone who can help you deal with what you have experienced. If your child is the one who sees everything negatively, give the situation some thought. Talk with your ex if possible and try to get to the bottom of it. If nothing seems to help, your child might be suffering from depression. Find a mental health professional who is experienced in working with children and get some outside help. You could also see a counselor with your child to help sort out what is happening and how you can improve things. (See Chapter 8 for information about what to do if the parenting schedule you have is simply not working and is causing problems for your child.)

For the most part, you can expect that things will slowly improve in the months and years after the divorce or separation. You might find that there are some changes you can make to your life, to the visitation schedule, or to the way in which you deal with the other parent that can make huge improvements in the way you and your child view the world. It could be as simple as altering the time visitation starts or ends or agreeing not to discuss schedule changes in front of your child. Later chapters discuss these possibilities in greater detail.

SYMPTOMS OF DEPRESSION IN CHILDREN

- Persistent sad or irritable mood
- Loss of interest in activities once enjoyed
- Significant change in appetite or body weight
- Difficulty sleeping or oversleeping
- Psychomotor agitation or retardation
- Loss of energy
- Feelings of worthlessness or inappropriate guilt
- Difficulty concentrating
- Recurrent thoughts of death or suicide
- Frequent vague, non-specific physical complaints, such as headaches, muscle
- aches, stomachaches, or tiredness
- Frequent absences from school or poor performance in school
- Talk of or efforts to run away from home
- Outbursts of shouting, complaining, unexplained irritability, or crying
- Being bored
- Lack of interest in playing with friends

- Alcohol or substance abuse
- Social isolation
- Poor communication
- Fear of death
- Extreme sensitivity to rejection or failure
- Increased irritability, anger, or hostility
- Reckless behavior
- Difficulty with relationships

(The National Institute of Mental Health, National Institute of Health Publication No. 00-4744)

Anger and Resentment

There's enough anger and resentment to go around after a divorce for sure. Both you and your child might feel some sort of anger or resentment toward each other and towards the other parent. This is normal. All families experience this at times. When you first discover that your child is angry with you, it may come as a great shock. It really is a normal part of the adjustment process though so don't let it get to you.

Some children are frightened by their own feelings and unable to understand or verbalize what they are really experiencing. You are not a therapist; you are a parent. No one expects you to be able to handle these feelings perfectly. Of course it hurts you to think your child is angry. Of course it just makes you even angrier at the other parent and at yourself. Of course it makes you sick to think that your child may blame himself or herself for the divorce, separation, or parenting plan scenario. You might also feel angry with your child about the way he or she is treating you. Your reaction is normal and so is your child's.

The first thing to do, even if you are a person who does not often talk about feelings, is to tell your child flat out that absolutely none of this is his or her fault and that nothing could have been done to change any of it. Children do not automatically know this. They need to be told. You will need to tell your child this on many occasions before it will really sink in. You need to tell your child that you love him or her very much and that nothing will ever change that. Reassure your child that you will always be a part of his or her life, and that the other parent will as well. Tell your child that it is perfectly fine for him or her to be angry at you, at the other parent, and at the world if necessary. Say that you want your child to tell you about anything that bothers him or her. You need to really listen to what your child says. Try not to categorize or define the feelings for him or her, and let them come out and accept them without judgment.

Next, open up a little bit about yourself. Tell your child that you are sorry that there was a divorce or end of the relationship and that it has been hard for you, too. Stress though that it is not your child's fault and he or she didn't make it happen and couldn't have changed it in any way.

Finding Out What Your Child Thinks

If you've read all of this and thought you aren't really sure how your child feels, do some detective work. Talk to your child's teacher. Younger kids especially are likely to blurt things out at school. Assuming you have access to your child's social media accounts and texts, see what he or she is saying there. This can provide a clear window to what your child is going through.

It's also a good idea to just check in with your kid and say "I want to know what you're thinking. How are you feeling? Tell me what you think right now about the situation."

Do Not Say Anything Bad about the Other Parent

When you talk to your child, talk about your own feelings, only. Your child needs to know that this has been hard for you too, but your child also needs to know that you are going to move forward and that you will always have lots of time and space in your life for him or her. Don't dwell on what you are going through. You are talking to your child, not a friend or confidant. This is not a time for you to explain what the other parent did wrong or why you got divorced or separated. Also be careful about what you say on social media where your child may see it. It can be confusing if you are saying to your child "your dad is a great guy; it just didn't work out with us" and then you're listing all of your ex's faults on Facebook where your child is your friend.

Emphasize that what happened with the other parent had only to do with your marriage or relationship. Explain that he or she will always be the child's mom or dad, and that you will always support that. It is also important to say that you are all still a family, but in a different way.

While all of the above might sound pretty simplistic and more appropriate for younger children, teens need to get this same message from you. Your teen may not be willing to discuss these things, but they are things that you need to say and they need to hear.

Don't expect this talk to be a cure-all. Instead, see it as a beginning. Keep the lines of communication open and try to find a way to talk about problems and feelings instead of yelling about them or closing up. It takes a lot of time to work through these things and there is no quick fix.

Social Media

If your child is friends with your or follows your social media accounts, monitor what you say there about the other parent, parenting, your emotions, and the entire situation. Consider saving the heavy stuff for direct interactions with your friends, or in online groups away from your child's eyes.

Social media is also something to watch closely for your child. In addition to being a way for your child to honestly express what he or she is feeling, social media can, at times, make things worse. Watch for bullying and interactions that add to your child's sense of isolation or depression.

When Your Child Blames You

There may be a time when your child or teen says something such as, "I hate you," or "I wish you weren't my mom/dad." These are difficult words to hear, but they are fairly common. Don't panic! Hearing your child say something like this hurts, but remember that your child doesn't truly mean it. In the heat of the moment it sounds pretty believable, but you have to remember that your child is, in fact, just a child. Teens may seem fairly adult sometimes, but they, too are struggling with their emotions.

Don't expect your child to have a mature reaction or take the time to really process his or her feelings in a complicated way. The best way to handle this is either to not react at all or to calmly say, "I'm sorry you feel that way." Don't try to get into a lengthy discussion or try to convince your child he or she is wrong. This really will pass. It is a temporary and very common reaction.

Your child may also say something at some point indicating that he or she blames you entirely for the divorce or separation. This is also common. Preteens and teens sometimes reach a point where they decide they have the entire situation figured out and can assign blame to one parent. This is a tough period to work through. Stay remain calm, even though inside you are furious that your child thinks this way (or in your opinion, has been brainwashed to think this way). You can tell your child that a divorce or separation is never one person's fault and there are always many reasons for it that only the people who were in the situation could ever truly understand. It takes two people to make a marriage work and two people to get a divorce. Don't get into all the reasons why you believe the other parent is at fault.

Dealing with the Fear of Abandonment

Your child has lost his or her nuclear family. One or both parents have moved to new residences. You and the other parent have decided that you don't want to live together anymore. Your child may naturally fear that you and the other parent may decide that you don't love him or her next. Even teens have this kind of subconscious fear. Everything in your child's universe has been substantially altered. Think for a moment how terrifying that is.

Let your child know that you are not abandoning him or her. You and the other parent have decided to change some things about where and how you live, and it has nothing to do with the child. He or she has a home at both places now, and there will always be a place for him or her.

Neither parent can ever decide not to love their child. Explain that there is a difference in the way moms and dads love each other and the way they love their kids. Parents choose each other and decide to live together. They can decide not to live together. Parents and kids do not choose each other and cannot decide they don't want to be together anymore. They're stuck!

Loving a spouse is like wearing a hat. You can take it off if you want to, if you have to, or if it gets uncomfortable. Loving a child is like having a head. You can never take it off, get rid of it, or truly change it. It is a part of you always. If your child is a teen, this explanation is too basic. Tell your child that people in a marriage can change how they feel, but that parents cannot change how they feel about their children. Remember that your child or teen does not know what loving a child feels like. Explain how it makes you feel and how it is a part of you that can never change.

If you filed for residential custody and your child is old enough to know this and wonder about it, help your child understand that you were not trying to keep the child away from the other parent when you asked for this. Explain that a child has to have one home, and it seemed to you and to the judge (and to the other parent if he or she agreed with this) that the best place for this home was with you. He or she still has two parents and will continue to have a home with both of you.

Some children feel a little lost when they begin to spend time alone with each parent on a scheduled basis. Even teens have a hard time adjusting. Make sure your child can reach you and the other parent at all times (this might mean getting your child a cell phone before an age that you had established). Having access to both parents all the time will help ease the transition and keep everyone connected. Work with your ex to establish the fact that your child can call or text either of you at any time.

You can help your child feel more comfortable with the schedule by explaining in advance what will happen. Make sure he or she knows where he or she will be and for how long. Be aware that as children grow older, they may have different reactions to the parenting schedule. Just because your child settles in and accepts the plan initially does not mean that problems will not arise with it down the line. It has to be a work in progress for everyone involved.

Dealing with Divided Loyalties

Children of divorce often feel pulled in two directions. They want to take both parents' sides. When with one parent, they will say bad things about the other. They want to please whomever they are with. Children feel confused and angry. The best way to cope with divided loyalties is to acknowledge they are going to happen and not encourage them. Never discuss your unpleasant feelings or opinions about the other parent with the child. Do not try to get your child to see your side of the story. Do not try to convince the child that you are right and the other parent is wrong. And don't latch onto what your child tells you as a reason to try to make a change. Your child might be telling you he would much rather not have to see the other parent while at the same time he's telling the other parent he wants to move in over there. And it's not that your child is lying either – it's likely your kid means what he says at the time he says it, but also means what he says to the other parent. Try not to get too hung up on this if possible.

The best way to try to handle this is not to have "sides" at all when it comes to parenting. Your children have two parents who love them, but who disagree about some things. The disagreements are not something the children need to be involved in or concern themselves with. If your child expresses opinions about the other parent, be available to listen, but do not become involved with the conflict by intervening, agreeing with the child, or criticizing the other parent. Talk to the other parent about this and see if you can both agree not to do these things. If the other parent does try to play on the divided loyalties, you should not do so in retaliation. Stand your ground. (Read more about this in Chapter 5.)

Dealing with Your Changing Feelings

Realize that you are going to experience changes in the way you feel as your new life as a residential parent plays out. There are going to be hard days when your child is with the other parent and you feel like you will simply die if you cannot see your child. You can get through these days by taking it one moment at a time. Look forward to the next time you will be together or think about good times you've had in the past. Distract yourself with work, friends, or family. Alcohol (or drugs) will not help you distract yourself, and will only make the entire situation worse and endanger your relationship with your child. There will also be days where you are happy to find yourself with the freedom to go anywhere and do anything without parenting obligations. You are not a bad parent for enjoying some freedom. It can be a welcome relief in the middle of the stressful adjustments you're living through.

You may find that your feelings towards your child may change. Some days you will feel like you know everything about your child, and other days he or she may be like a stranger who has a whole other life that you are excluded from. This is actually very natural. If your child is school age, remember when she started school and suddenly you had no idea what she was doing all day? You were out of the loop and felt a little distanced from your child's life at school. This is a similar situation. Your child has time with the other parent that you aren't part of. There's no way to change that, so the best option is to try to support and embrace it.

When you feel very connected and comfortable, let your child know. Give hugs, say how happy you are feeling, or just enjoy it. If you feel excluded, ask questions and make conversation so you can feel included, but never accuse your child of leaving you out or cutting you off. You want to convey positive or constructive feelings whenever possible. If your child (or more likely teen!) really is trying to exclude you, calmly explain that you would like to be involved in his or her life or activities. Discuss it without placing blame on the child.

All of your feelings are real and important, but they are not all appropriate to share with your child. Confide in a friend or relative, but keep your child off the emotional roller coaster that you may find yourself on.

There will be times when you are angry with your child. This does not make you a bad parent. Before the marriage or relationship ended, there were times when you became angry with your child. It is normal to have this happen occasionally. Be certain that you control your anger, but feel free to be human and express it reasonably.

Dealing with Your Child's Changing Feelings

Just as you are on an emotional roller coaster, so is your child. One day he or she refuses to go with the other parent and the next day he or she demands to go there house. Your best bet is to not react in the heat of the moment. Count to ten if you have to before reacting. Be loving and supportive. This does not mean that anything your child does can be excused because of the trauma of divorce or separation. There are standards of behavior that your child must meet and as the parent, you are the one to set them and enforce them. You can give some leeway when needed, but you cannot allow a child's emotions to control you or your life. Chapter 4 deals with this in-depth. Just keep in mind that all of these extreme moods cannot-and do not-last forever. Stick to your schedule and do not give in.

Many experts compare the divorce or separation adjustment process with the grieving process. Understand that your child has many stages and phases to go through—just as you do—in order to accept what has happened. Children often have delayed reactions to divorce or separation. They may not scream and shout when you tell them about the divorce or separation the first time. It may take months for their emotions to fully develop about the situation. As children grow older, they begin to process the divorce or separation differently and may have different reactions with each passing year. Be ready for issues to pop up at any time now or in the future.

Be Patient

If you find that you need help dealing with your child's emotions, there are many things you can do.

- Talk to the other parent first, if possible. Compare notes and see if you can devise a solution together. Working together is always the best way to address parenting problems.
- Talk to a counselor or therapist. You can see a counselor alone and get some ideas for how to cope without having to involve your child in counseling, or you can have your child meet with a counselor if you like.

- Talk to your child's teacher. Teachers can often offer insights about a child's behavior.

Remember that children's emotions are not always clear and they are not easily categorized. Talk about what is in front of you, but realize there may be more to it than you are hearing. Learn to ask noncritical, open-ended questions that will help draw your child out and bring a wide range of emotions to the forefront. Do not be afraid to get help from counselors or therapists.

Learn to roll with the punches when it comes to dealing with emotions. Try to be responsive in an intelligent and thoughtful way. If your child is being clingy, you may want to change your plans to take him to a get-together with your friends. If she is determined to be angry with you, you might want to get out of the house and do something to take both your minds off the situation or you might decide to just let him or her spend the afternoon gaming or listening to music. Be prepared to be flexible. Remember that you have feelings as well, and sometimes they are going to clash with your child's feelings. You are not going to handle all of this perfectly and no one expects you to. Be yourself and try to put parenting first on your list of priorities.

Chapter 3

Communicating with Your Child

Once you are living with a parenting schedule that limits your time with your child, it can become harder to feel as if you are communicating well. While you are adjusting to the new schedule, pay careful attention to how you are communicating. Eventually things will become easier and you won't need to constantly monitor what you say or how you say it. Even though you may feel as though you haven't really changed and so your relationship with your child should not change, divorce changes everything.

You are going through a difficult time and it may be hard to control your emotions in a time with so much turmoil. However, this is something you have to do for the sake of your child. It may seem too much to expect that you have to put your child first when you probably feel like nobody has put you first in a long time. But it will be worth it.

There may also be times in the years ahead when it seems as though communication with your child is breaking down. If you can take a few months and pay attention to your communications with your child, you will find that you can rebuild some bonds you might have thought were lost or damaged. Always keep in mind that communication problems may be the result of normal changes and isn't always caused by the divorce. Ask any parent of a teen and they will tell you it's not easy to communicate. Add in the complications of a divorce or separation and it can be a complex situation. Come back to this chapter then and review the suggestions in times of need. You and your child have a long road ahead that you need to walk together. Building your communication and trust today can only help you in the years ahead.

What to Say to Your Child

Of course you know how to talk to your child, but it can be helpful to have some things firmly in your mind that you need to communicate.

- **Say the unsaid.** After a divorce, verbalize things that you normally would not need to say. You might thing you don't need to tell your child "I could never hate you" or "You will always have two parents." But after divorce, your child needs to hear these things.
- **Remember to praise.** Tell your child how proud you are when he or she succeeds at something. Remind your child that he or she is good at certain things.
- **Talk about the divorce.** Do so without getting angry about the other parent. Answer questions. Be honest if you don't know the answers.
- **Don't talk about the divorce too much.** Let your child be your guide. When he or she asks questions or brings it up, talk about it, but don't get up each morning and say, "So how are you feeling about the divorce today?"
- **Be sincere.** Don't say what you think you should. Say what you mean and what is important to you. You have to be yourself, no matter what.
- **Be honest.** Being honest does not mean being harsh, overly detailed, or very negative, even when talking about the divorce. But you shouldn't sugarcoat things, either. There's a delicate balance to honesty where you tell the truth but don't share too much.
- **Focus on the present.** Talk to your child about his or her life and activities. Be involved in his or her day-to-day life and recognize it is

important. You cannot change what has happened, but you can help your child know that you are still and will always be involved in his or her life. Being a part of the small parts of your child's life will mean a lot to him or her. While you might be thinking about the divorce all the time and working through the emotions and questions you have, kids need to focus on what they are doing today most of the time. Stay grounded with them.

- **Be positive about the other parent.** Emphasize the good in the other parent, even if you aren't really sold on it yourself. Be happy when your child has a good time with the other parent, not resentful.

THINGS TO SAY TO YOUR CHILD
- I love you.
- You are always going to be part of my family.
- I'm happy to be with you today.
- I am so proud of the way you_____. (fill in the blank)
- I know this is difficult for you.
- I am always willing to listen to anything you need to talk about.
- This is your home, and Mom's/Dad's house is your home as well.
- Your mother/father and I disagree about some things and that's okay.
- Mom/Dad and I divorced each other, but not you. We will always be your parents and we will work hard to be parents together.
- Moms and dads can get divorced, but parents and kids never can.
- Your Mom/Dad will always be your Mom/Dad. That's how I want it.
- This is the schedule we are going to be using. I'd like to know how you feel about it.

- When we are not together, I think about you and am happy to know I will be seeing you again soon.
- You can call Mom/Dad anytime you want to.
- How did (fill in the blank) go at school today?
- What did you do at your friend's house yesterday?
- What would you like to do tonight?
- We're using this schedule because we think it is the best way to share our time with you. We both would be with you all the time if we could, but we can't.
- We're not going to get back together. I know that would make you happy, but the divorce is final and we won't change our minds.
- Why don't you ask Mom/Dad to help you with that. He/she is good at things like that.
- Mom/Dad loves you and always has.
- It isn't anyone's fault that we got divorced. Sometimes marriages just don't work out.
- How great that Mom/Dad took you to the zoo. What did you see there?
- I think that if you are upset about what happened at Mom's/Dad's house, you should talk to her/him about it.

Things You Should Not Say

You aren't perfect, so there are going to be things that fly out of your mouth sometimes without thinking. It's okay to be human and you can't beat yourself up about it. But you can try to keep in mind the kinds of conversations and comments that will not be very helpful to your child.

- **Don't say bad things about the other parent.** Think about how hurt you would be if someone criticized someone you love. That's how your child feels when you say bad things about the other parent. It's okay to let your child know that you and the other parent have differences, but it is not okay to insult, demean, or degrade the other parent. You know what he or she has done wrong, but keep it to yourself.

- **Don't suggest that your child must choose between you.** Children want to please both parents and can often end up in a tailspin trying to make both parents happy.
- **Don't share your personal details.** You should keep the adult details of the divorce, your turmoil, and your emotions to yourself Your child is not a friend or a shoulder to lean on. Adult information is only for adults. Don't talk about your loneliness, your heartache, your anger, or your sadness. Use friends and family for those topics.
- **Don't talk about money.** Don't get your child involved in your financial problems. It's okay to explain you cannot afford something, but it is not okay to detail what exactly you got in the divorce and how you can't survive with the child support payments you're getting.
- **Don't ask your child to spy or carry messages.** Your child is not a go-between and should never be asked to tell the other parent something or even deliver a note. The child is subject to the other parent's emotional reaction and will feel as if the anger is meant for him or her. Your child is not a spy who can keep you up to date on the other parent's life and should not be asked to bring back reports.
- **Don't make promises you can't keep.** It is easy to sometimes say things out of wishful thinking, but your child needs promises he or she can rely on.
- **Don't pry for details.** It's good to talk with your child about what he or she did with the other parent. It's an important part of his or her life and it shouldn't be something that is taboo to discuss. But don't start prying for details or get too involved in finding out exactly what happened. The information you get is not going to be very accurate since children's perceptions are skewed by their own self-interest.

THINGS NOT TO SAY TO YOUR CHILD

- Your mother/father is dishonest/mean/stupid/cruel/lazy/cheap, etc.
- You're going to have to choose which parent you want to be with.
- Wouldn't you rather be with me this weekend? We could do anything you wanted.
- You always side with your mother/father.
- You are just like your mother/father.
- Ever since the divorce I have felt so alone.
- Don't tell Mom/Dad we did this.
- Which one of us do you love more?
- I want you to know that this is all your mother's/father's fault.
- When you leave, I am all alone.
- Don't you wish you could see me more?
- It's okay if you don't want to go to Mom's/Dad's. You don't have to go.
- Sometimes I just want to kill myself
- We can't go to the movies because your mother/father took all the money from me in the divorce.
- Who was that man/woman at the house when I picked you up?
- Where is Mom/Dad going tonight?
- I don't get enough child support to buy you a new coat.
- I have to get a job because Mom/Dad doesn't give us enough money to live on.
- Tell Mom/Dad you need to be home by 7 instead of 8.
- If your mother/father didn't waste all her/his money on shoes/beer, I might get enough child support to buy you the new _ you want.
- Tell your mother/father I need that check by Friday or I'm taking her/him to court.
- You always have an attitude when you come back from there.

- You should tell Mom/Dad that you love me more.
- It is disgusting that he/she bought a new car and I don't have enough to pay for your school lunches.
- Watch out for men/women. They take what they want and throw you aside.
- Don't ever get married. You'll regret it.
- You can just tell him/her that if you aren't home on time next week, I'm calling the police.

Listening to Your Child

To truly communicate with your child, you need to listen to what he or she is telling you, verbally and nonverbally. Pay attention to his or her reactions to things and draw conclusions.

- **Ask open-ended questions to get your child to open up.** Show interest in the things he or she is doing and thinking about. Listen to what he or she is talking about and respond.
- **Expect children under age 8 to ask repeated questions about the divorce or separation,** the schedule, the other parent, etc. Answer these questions even if you feel as if you already did. The repetition will show the child that this new world he or she is living in is dependable.
- **Listen to requests for change.** Your child may, at some point, say he or she would rather live with the other parent. Usually this happens when a conflict arises in your home, but it is also common from an older child who is the same sex as the other parent. Find out why your child is asking before becoming defensive. There are times when a change of custody is appropriate, but often this request is your child's way of pointing out a problem or bonding with the other parent.
- **Understand that your child may say one thing and mean another.** It is common for your child's emotions about the divorce and new

schedule to come out in other ways, so be sensitive to the real reasons for things. A tantrum over bedtime may actually have something to do with all of the changes and not just the rules about bedtime.
- **Try not to superimpose your own assumptions onto your child.** Do not assume you know what she is feeling without getting some information first.
- **Understand that digital communication, while helpful, is limited.** Don't try to have deep and important conversations with your kid via text or messenger. It's too hard to misunderstand and you don't get the tone and subtext.

Chapter 4

Rules for Your Child

The most important thing for a child who has experienced a divorce or separation is normalcy. Children need to feel that, although their parents' relationship has drastically changed, many things in their own lives will remain stable. It is crucial now more than ever that your child feels there are things in life that he or she can count on.

One of the best ways to help a child feel rooted, protected, and loved is to have rules. Think about what life was like when you and the other parent lived together. You had a set of rules your child was expected to follow. In most families, these rules are unspoken, but everyone understands what they are. Children usually have some chores they are responsible for; there are set times for things such as meals, baths, and homework; and, there is behavior and speech that is not acceptable.

Now that you and the other parent have divorced or separated, it's important that your child continue to have rules and responsibilities. Life goes on, and maintaining rules and continuing to expect certain things will demonstrate this to your child. The tricky part in all of this is that the rules may need to change a bit because of the change in all of your lives. Making those changes without letting chaos ensue is where the challenge comes in.

Some parents feel as if they should give their child a break. After all, he or she has been through a lot and expecting him or her to take out the garbage or clean the rabbit cage seems like an extra burden. But continuing to live normal lives where everyone has responsibilities and jobs is the best way to help your child get on track with the new situation. Life isn't carefree and easy, and you can't pretend that it is. Of course, it is fine to make exceptions to the rules, but you need to have the rules or your everyday life will just fall apart. Your relationship or marriage might have ended, but life has to go on and you've got to have rules to keep it all together in your household.

To Parents with Sole Custody

You will notice that in this section and in other parts of the book, it is recommended that you and the other parent try to work together as parents, making rules and decisions about your child together. If you have legal sole custody (see Chapter 1 for an explanation of the different types of custody), you are not legally obligated to do this. However, you should know that even if you're the one with the legal authority, it's still important to keep the other parent involved in your child's life and to try to work together to create rules for your child that will apply at both homes.

If you were given sole decision-making power by the court, there's probably a good reason for that. If you feel that you do not wish to include the other parent in the decision-making process, that is your right and you may be completely justified in this regard. You need to assess your situation and determine if it is possible to include the other parent in any decisions at all. If it is not, then focus on encouraging and developing your child's relationship with the other parent, while making sure that you handle the major decisions (such as medical care, religion, schooling, and other activities).

While you can't control what happens at the other parent's home, the best way to impact what happens there is to talk about it calmly and rationally with the other parent. The other parent is free to create rules at his or her own home (within reason and that do not cause harm to the child), and you can't demand to be part of that decision-making process. For example, if your four-year-old has a bedtime of 8 o'clock at your home, but the other parent allows her to stay up until 9:30 p.m., you aren't going to be able to make the other parent change this. You can, however, point out that your child is tired and cranky the next day, and suggest that the other parent talk with the preschool teacher to learn how it is impacting the child at school.

Whose Rules: Yours or the Other Parent's

In an ideal world, the family and household rules that were in place before the divorce or separation are the rules that you should continue to use. This will give your child a sense of continuity and will also lessen the potential for disagreement with your child and with the other parent.

In reality, most parents find that they do need to make changes to house rules after a divorce. Schedules change, as do the children's emotional needs, and nothing can ever be as it was. You may feel that since you are now the only parent in your household, you should be able to set the rules in your household. If you feel this way, you are right to a certain extent. It is your home, and you can decide how you will live and what the rules will be in your house.

Taking responsibility for your own rules is an important part of coping with divorce. However, it's important to remember that your child now has two homes to live in and two parents to obey separately. It's just simpler if the rules in both homes are the same or very similar, particularly if your child is very young. Coordinating in this way lets your child know that you and the other parent will continue to parent together and that there is still a family unit that has importance in the child's life. It's much easier for your child to transition from one home to the next if the basic schedule and responsibilities in each home are relatively the same. It creates less of an adjustment each time your child moves between homes.

Creating Rules Together

Arrange to speak to the other parent (when your child is not around) and say you would like to discuss the rules that your child will be following in both homes. Explain that you believe it makes sense for both of you to have rules for your child that are the same or similar and you would like to work together to create rules that will work in both homes. You could show the other parent the information in the other half of this book to help explain the importance.

RULES TO DISCUSS WITH THE OTHER PARENT
- Bedtime
- Wake-up time
- How often bathing should occur
- When homework should be done
- Household chores (there will be differences between the households, but the main point is that there should be some at each home and the time and difficulty level should be similar)
- Unacceptable behavior, language, and attitudes from your child
- Screen time limits
- Unacceptable foods or limits on certain foods for your child (For example, some doctors recommend limiting daily juice intake in babies, toddlers, and preschoolers. There are similar recommendations for soda intake for older children and teens. Some children have food allergies, while others have religious restrictions on diet.)
- School attendance
- When medication must be taken
- Limits on types of gaming, social media, and online activity that is acceptable at each age
- The standard by which the child must keep his or her room clean

- Church and religious class attendance
- When friends may come over and when the child may visit friends
- Curfew
- Teeth brushing, flossing, and other hygiene
- Naps (for younger children)
- Anything else either of you feel is important

The goal is to try to keep most of the rules the same at both homes, but you and the other parent will probably find that some rules need adjustments. It's also important to remember that you may not agree about all of the rules. In that case, you will need to compromise – you could decide one rule and the other parent could decide another, or else you could reach a decision on a rule that is halfway between the two opinions (an 8:30 bedtime if one person says 8:00 and one says 9:00). You may also realize that some rules need to be different in each home. If this is what you both agree will work best, then it's fine. If you absolutely cannot reach an agreement or compromise, then you will each have to set your own rules.

You will probably gradually reach a point where you don't need to discuss certain rules. You aren't going to be spending the rest of your lives negotiating rules with the other parent. Eventually, things will evolve to a point where most things are understood and don't require long discussions. As your child grows up and reaches new milestones (starting school, getting braces, getting his or her driver's license, getting a job, beginning to date, joining a sports team, and so on), it will be helpful to talk with the other parent about rules again, so you can coordinate with each other about rules for the changing situation.

Discussing Rules with Your Child

If most of the rules will remain the same as before the divorce or separation, it probably won't be necessary for you to have a formal conversation with your child about them. Just make them a part of your daily life when the child is at your home. If something will be changing, discuss it with your child. It is likely there will be different rules for some things at each home. Help your child understand and adjust to this. Some parents find that it is useful to post the house rules at each home, especially if you have a child that has trouble handling rules.

SAMPLE HOUSE RULES LIST

- We do not yell at each other or hit each other.
- We always treat each other with respect and kindness.
- Bedtime is at 9:00 p.m. on school nights and 9:30 p.m. on other nights.
- Dirty laundry is to be placed in the hamper.
- Everyone must clear his or her own dishes off the table.
- _____ is responsible for folding all of the laundry.
- Every Tuesday night the hamster cage will be cleaned out by _____.
- Homework must be done before screen time.
- If you spill it, you clean it up.
- All beds must be made before breakfast.
- We will take turns loading the dishwasher.
- Whoever is home on Saturday morning will help clean the house.
- There is a half hour limit on gaming time on weeknights.

Some younger children benefit from a sticker chart, where the child gets a sticker placed on the chart for each chore that is done or every rule that is followed that day. If the child receives a sticker in each category for a day or a week, a small reward can help reinforce the behavior.

SAMPLE STICKER CHART

Cara's Sticker Chart	Mon	Tues	Wed	Thurs	Fri	Sat	Sun
Put away her toys							
Did not throw anything							
Brushed her teeth							
Played nicely with dog							
Carried her dishes to the sink							
Washed her hands before eating							
Placed her shoes beside her bed							
Was quiet while adults were talking							

Some parents of teens find they like to have a contract with their child. A contract makes the teen take an active role in acknowledging and agreeing to the rules.

SAMPLE CONTRACT WITH A TEEN

Chase White and his father Tom White enter into this contract and agree to follow it for the next four months.

The parties agree that they will not swear or shout.

On the days Chase is home, he will take out the trash, make his bed, and help do the dishes.

Chase will do his homework before he goes out with friends or uses technology.

Chase will set his alarm and make sure he is on time for school.

> Chase will be home by 11 p.m. on weekends when he is home. If he is late, he will be grounded the next weekend day he is here.
>
> Chase will not ride in a car with an unlicensed driver.
>
> Chase will not have female guests over when Dad is not home.
>
> Chase will earn $20 for every grade higher than a B on his report card.
>
> Dad will not work on Sundays when Chase is home and will spend the day with him instead.
>
> _____ _____ _____ _____
> Chase Williams   date   Thomas Williams   date

The contract contains all of the rules and consequences the teen must follow. Both parents and the child sign it and agree to follow it. Sometimes these contracts also list what responsibilities the parents are committing to (listening to the child without judgment, attending the child's sporting or extracurricular events, and providing transportation to outings with friends, etc.).

Creating Your Own Rules

Because you now live on your own and your lifestyle has changed, there will be situations that arise at your home that were never an issue when you lived as a family. For example, your child may now arrive after school to an empty house. You will need rules to deal with situations like these. You don't need to initiate a discussion about these decisions with the other parent, since they happen at your house, unless you would like to get some input. Realize that the other parent may hear about these changes and wish to discuss them with you. Don't view this as an attempt by the other parent to question your authority or undermine you. Briefly and calmly give a simple explanation. The other parent's involvement in your child's life is a good thing.

The Other Parent's Rules

The flip side to this is that things have changed for the other parent as well. He or she may find it necessary to formulate some new rules that pertain to new situations that are happening at that home. You may hear things from your child that concern you. Calmly ask the other parent about these new situations and rules so that you can be informed before you jump to conclusions. Remember that you have no authority to dictate what the rules will be in the other home, but you do have the right to understand them so you can know what your child is doing, and so you can support the rules. It's also important that you do not question the basis for these rules in front of your child.

As a parent, your job is to help your child obey and live with rules, no matter who has created them and whether they are right or wrong. You would not suggest to your child that his or her teacher is wrong and that a rule at school shouldn't be obeyed because you don't agree with it. You need to respect the other parent's rules in the same way.

Rules That Are Wrong

You and the other parent clearly have different opinions about some things—that's why you're no longer together. Occasions will arise where you feel the other parent has made a rule that is wrong. The best way to handle this is to discuss it with him or her when your child is not present. It's also important to step back and evaluate just how important this is.

If the other parent has a rule that your child must vacuum his or her room when he or she arrives at the other home, and you feel that it is excessive, take a look at the situation. Is this rule going to do serious harm to your child? Just because a child is unhappy about a rule does not mean it is wrong.

If the other parent has a rule that the child may cross a busy street alone, and you believe the child is too young and could be harmed, then you do need to make an effort to get the other parent to change the rule by having a calm and reasonable discussion about it. (See Chapter 6 for more information about communicating with the other parent.) If you feel rules persist at the other home that are dangerous to your child or are completely unreasonable, you need to speak to your attorney or get outside help as discussed in Chapter 12. The same thing applies to discipline that you feel is dangerous or completely unreasonable.

Misinformation

When dealing with the other parent's rules, remember that what your child tells you may not be entirely correct or complete. Kids can twist things a bit, sometimes because their perceptions or memories are wrong and sometimes to get a reaction out of you. Before you fly off the handle, get the information from the other parent. Things usually aren't as bad as they sound, and even if something seems wrong on its face, an explanation from the other parent may show why it was necessary. You may also find your child did not give you all the details and left some important things out.

Bending the Rules

When you lived together as a family, there were times when the rules were bent or even completely thrown out the window. A special family gathering may have resulted in a late bedtime, a busy week may have meant household chores were skipped, and so on. Just because you are trying to provide continuity and stability does not mean you are a prison guard. It is perfectly fine to bend the rules and make exceptions, as long as you don't do it all the time. Flexibility is an important part of parenting.

Changing Rules for Your Changing Child

If your child is 8 years old and has an 8:30 p.m. bedtime, soon he or she will be older and able to stay up later. As children get older, many things in their lives change: amount of homework, curfew, screen time limits, eating habits, sleep needs, time with friends, etc. Rules for some of these things just gradually change with the child.

Other times, you need to formally change a rule. When you notice that a rule needs to be changed, try to discuss it with the other parent. He or she has probably noticed the same thing and both of you have probably begun to make adjustments. As your child gets older, and as the trauma of the divorce or separation gets farther into the past, your child will be more comfortable with the notion of two homes, and having some rules that are different at each home will no longer be as difficult to handle. You will eventually reach a point where things are run one way at your home and another way at the other parent's home, and it is no longer a problem for anyone.

When Rules Are Broken

Part of having rules is having consequences when they are broken. When you and the other parent meet to discuss what the basic rules will be, you need to discuss the appropriate types of repercussions for broken rules. Some parents find it helpful to write these down. You should agree that you won't question the other parent's use of these consequences and will not interfere with them. It is important to discuss whether punishments will apply at both homes. For example, if your teen breaks curfew at your home and is grounded by you for three days, will this be three consecutive days and apply at whichever home the child is at or will it only apply to the next three days the child is at your home? You need to decide together how to handle these situations.

It is also important to note that mental health experts generally discourage the use of physical punishment. Physical punishment is never a good idea and can be especially dangerous when you have a former spouse on the lookout for child abuse. Protect yourself and your child and avoid physical punishment.

Final Thoughts about Rules

When you and your child are first adjusting to life after divorce or separation, there will be conflict about rules and the child will find many opportunities to tell you that you are being unfair or that your rules are not the same as the other parent's. Also, as your child grows older, he or she may complain that some rules are now unfair. This is normal (you probably felt the same way about your own parents' rules whether you grew up in one house or two). It's part of adjusting and part of growing up. Your job is to hold steady and not give in, unless you truly believe a rule needs to be changed. Make sure you take the time to talk to your child about rules and listen to and consider his or her input. Eventually, you will find that you get into a routine where every little rule is no longer questioned. Don't give up just because things get rocky. Your child will love and respect you more if you have consistent and fair rules that are evenly applied, even if he or she squawks in the short term. Keep in mind that in order for your child to grow up believing that he or she is still part of a family and that he or she has two parents who love and believe in him or her, you need to demonstrate respect and consideration for the other parent. Even if you believe he or she has random rules and ineffective punishments, don't tell your child. Be a model for your child by showing him or her that it is important to treat other people with respect and consideration (despite their behaviors), and that rules must be followed no matter how random or wrong they seem. Encourage your child to voice his or her opinion about rules, but remind him or her that parents make the rules. You and the other parent are still parenting together, and in order to do so you must support each other's decisions, rules, and consequences.

TIPS FOR MAKING RULES THAT WORK

- Consult with the other parent so that both homes have similar expectations.
- Choose rules that are in tune with your lifestyle and expectations.
- Apply rules consistently and use fair, consistent consequences.
- Expect to change your rules as your child changes.
- Realize you cannot control the environment at the other parent's home, but that you can control yours.

Chapter 5

Rules for Yourself

In order for your parenting plan to work you have to consciously make an effort to make it work. Just because you are now divorced and living by yourself as a single parent does not mean that things are going to be free and easy for you. Things are going to be difficult for a while until you, your child, and the other parent have adjusted to your new lives. To get through the difficult adjustment period and create a plan for the future, you need to have some rules for yourself. There may also be times in the future when things will become difficult. Return to this chapter then to help yourself cope.

Deal with Your Emotions

You have a lot to cope with in terms of your feelings of loss, anger, frustration, depression, love, grief, and fear. Allow yourself to recognize what you are feeling and work through them. Suppressing and denying your feelings is not the answer. However, you do have to find a way to control your emotions around your child and the other parent. You and your child should focus on maintaining your relationship, not on rehashing the divorce. Your feelings about the divorce or separation are for you to deal with. Your child has an enormous amount of emotions to handle without trying to cope with or understand yours. Resolve to control your emotions the best you can when around your child. That being said, be authentic. It's ok to be sad, to show you are struggling, and to be human. Just try to do all of that without placing the burden of fixing it on your child.

You and the other parent are no longer emotional partners and you must separate yourself from him or her emotionally, while continuing to parent together.

TIPS FOR DEALING WITH YOUR EMOTIONS
- See a therapist or counselor.
- Confide in friends.
- Spend time thinking through your problems and challenges.
- Forgive yourself.
- Find joy in your time with your child.
- Do not expect to be perfect.
- Learn some anger management skills to help deal with the other parent if necessary.
- Remember that where you are today is now where you will be next month, next year, or in the next decade.

Work with the Other Parent
Some residential parents believe that because the court gave them sole or residential custody of their child that they have been appointed head parent. Parenting must always be a joint effort. Certainly, each parent will be in charge of the child at different times, but at no time is either parent in charge of the other parent. Thinking that you can direct the other parent to do things, change his or her behavior, or tell him or her what he or she can or cannot do with the child will only lead to trouble. It's just not worth your time to try.

Try to adopt a cooperative approach to the other parent. Don't think of him or her as the enemy, a less capable parent, or someone who needs your guidance (even if that's the truth). Remember that you're not in charge of his or her parenting. You may be able to offer advice, but you can't assume it will be taken. It's best if you can find a way to communicate with each other, and share concerns and opinions about your child. This has to be done in a way that allows you to respect each other's parenting rights and give each other space. Don't act like the victor, the righteous, and the anointed best parent, even if you secretly believe this to be the case. Instead think of your role as being there to help the other parent do the best he or she can. The bottom line is your kid needs both parents. Make it your mission to make sure that your kid gets that.

If you want to have input into the way the other parent does things, you'll catch more flies with honey than vinegar. Offer suggestions, helpful hints, and information, but avoid sounding as if you are issuing commands, making demands, or laying down the law. Resolve to try to be polite and to keep negative thoughts to yourself.

Do Not Speak Negatively about the Other Parent

Your child has another parent and spends time with that parent. Don't pretend that the other parent doesn't exist. Your child will talk about the other parent because he or she is an important part of the child's life. Don't not stop your child from discussing the other parent and continuing to have a deep and meaningful relationship.

You should monitor what comes out of your own mouth about the other parent. Resolve to never say anything derogatory, insulting, cruel, or negative about the other parent in front of your child. That does not mean you can't think it; just don't say it.

Your child loves the other parent and will always have a relationship with him or her. You must allow this and it's not your role to get your child to see the other parent's "true colors." Be encouraging about the time the child spends with the other parent. Let him or her have a separate relationship with the other parent and allow him or her to draw his or her own conclusions.

Just as you must bite your tongue sometimes when speaking to the other parent (see Chapter 6 for guidelines about this), there are times when you need to bite your tongue around your child. Do not let negative comments about the other parent slip out. Never negatively compare your child to the other parent. ("You're thoughtless just like your mother.")

One common trap is talking about the other parent to your friends or family at a time when your child can overhear. It's easy to tell yourself this is ok because you're not talking to your child or that your child is probably not even paying attention. In truth, your kids pick up on what you're saying when you're in hearing distance, even if you're not talking to them. This means you have to censor yourself when your child could hear what you're saying. That can be hard when you really need to talk to someone.

It also means you have to be careful what you put on social media. Even if your child can't see what you post, other people can and it can get back to your child, particularly a media-savvy teen. Social media is part of your public face that your child can see. Try to make sure your words are not hurtful.

Talk to Your Child

When you're with your kid, don't talk all about yourself: what you are doing, what you are feeling, etc. Of course, you should share some of your thoughts and feelings in order to have a good relationship with your child, but it should not be all about you. Be yourself but hold back the parts that are about adult relationships.

When with your child, avoid talking about everything that went wrong in the relationship with the other parent and your longing for the past or your anger at how things ended. That being said, it's impossible to act as though the past never happened. It is normal and healthy to mention something that sparks a memory you share. ("That's just like the time we went camping and Dad got lost in the woods.") You have shared memories and it's normal to talk about them, whether they are happy or sad.

Try to avoid being overly critical of your child while you are all adjusting to your new lives or to a recent change in the situation. You are bound to be more irritable, more easily hurt, and more easily annoyed during this period.

Try to find a way to monitor what comes out of your mouth even as you are hurting and confused inside.

There will probably be a time when your child complains to you about the other parent. Resolve to listen to what the child has to say but do not become involved in the dispute. A good answer is to tell the child that you are glad he or she feels comfortable telling you about this, but that it is something he or she needs to discuss with the other parent. The exception is if your child is in danger or is extremely upset. (See Chapter 7 for information about how to intervene.)

Respect Parenting Time

Respecting your child's time with and feelings for the other parent is an important rule to make for yourself. Make sure that scheduled parenting time is a priority in your child's schedule. Support and encourage their relationship. This does not mean you have to be a cheerleader, but it does mean you should not discourage visitation or say negative things about the other parent. If you demonstrate that you respect that time, it will show your child you support their relationship and it will help your child feel secure and comfortable.

Avoid Confrontations

Avoid arguments and non productive discussions with the other parent, especially in front of your child. Try to be as civil as possible to the other parent at these times. It won't always be easy, but it will help your child. (See Chapter 6 for more about this.)

Talk Honestly, But Carefully about the Divorce

There will be times when your child will ask you questions about why you divorced and how you feel about the other parent. It is important to be honest, yet not unduly negative. Instead of saying, "Your mother is selfish and I couldn't put up with it anymore," or, "Your father was sleeping around," you should try to give an answer like, "Mom and I disagreed about a lot of things," or, "Dad and I decided that we wanted to live our lives differently." It is important to make it clear that neither parent is at fault and that you will not be getting back together. Resolve to answer questions honestly, but without unnecessary or hurtful details.

Make Real Promises to Your Child

Do not make promises you cannot keep. Period.

It is much better to be honest with your child. If your child does not want to go to spend time with the other parent, instead of promising that he or she will not have to go, explain why it is important for him or her to go. Say you miss your child when he's away, and that you are sad when you are apart, but that you focus on how happy it will be the next time you are together and how much fun he or she will have with the other parent. Make promises that are realistic. If you have to break a promise, be honest about it and tell your child right away. Explain what has happened and why you can't keep your promise.

If a child doesn't want to go because of issues with the other parent, it's not your job to resolve them. They have their own relationship and it's up to them to solve the problems. Parent-child relationships aren't always easy, but in working through the problems the parent and child become more attached and deepen their relationship. Step aside and let them find their way together. This can be hard if you were often the one moderating between the two when you all lived together, but the reality is that it's not your job anymore.

Decide Who You Are

One of the benefits of a divorce or separation is you get to reinvent yourself, or get back to who you truly are. It's a chance to explore new interests, make changes, and choose new paths. That can be scary, but it can also be fun and satisfying. It's up to you to define yourself from now on. Your child's parent doesn't get to decide you are. You can decide what kind of co-parent you're going to be, what kind of parent you're going to be, and what kind of ex you're going to be. It's all completely up to you. You have the freedom to change everything right now. Take advantage of it.

Be on Time
Set up parenting transfer times for times when you are available. Waiting at the window for your car to arrive for 45 minutes or sitting in the driveway with the other parent waiting for you to get home will upset your child and send a message that you don't care. Your child already probably has some feelings of abandonment. Don't make them worse. When you have made a commitment to being with your child, be on time. It is also important to be on time if you are dropping the child off at the other parent's home. Doing so will show the child and the other parent that you respect their relationship and support their time together.

Promise yourself that you will be on time. If you are going to be late for an unforeseen reason, call and let your child and the other parent know. If you find that you are regularly late, you may need to make some schedule changes.

Be Present
People talk about quality time versus quantity time. It sounds like a line, but it is true to some extent. The truth of the matter is you will now not see your child every single day. There will be weekends and possibly weeks when you are not together. It's hard and it's not ideal. What you can do is make the time you are together matter. This may mean setting rules limiting your own cell phone or tablet time when you are together. This might mean you push some things aside to do when your kid isn't around. If you can make the time you do have really count, you'll feel more satisfied.

Make the Best of It
Being a divorced or separated parent is nobody's dream—the dream is a happy and cozy little family where nobody has to divide time. But the fact of the

matter is that this is where you are, and you have to try find a way to live with it and make it work for you. Promise yourself from the beginning that you will make the most of the time you have with your child. This is different from setting unreasonably high expectations for yourself. It's not going to be perfect and it's not going to come easily. Give your child your full attention whenever possible, be emotionally available for your child and always look for the bright side. This doesn't mean you shouldn't have a life. You have a job, friends, and family, and you need to continue to live your life. You should not hole up in the house with your child. When you are active, happy, and fulfilled, you are a better parent. You do need to think about your child's emotions and remember to include your child in the new life you are building for yourself.

RULES TO LIVE BY

- Don't confide in your child about all of your feelings about the divorce or separation.
- Make real time for your child in your life.
- Respect your child's time with and feelings about the other parent.
- Be on time in all your dealings with your child.
- See yourself as emotionally separate from the other parent.
- Be honest about the fact that reconciliation is not going to happen.
- Find a way to cope with your emotions. See a therapist or talk with friends.
- Live your own life. To be a good parent, you must have your own life.
- Never speak negatively about the other parent in front of your child.
- Be yourself, but protect your child from your adult feelings.
- Enjoy the freedom and opportunities you have now instead of focusing on the negatives.

Parenting Together Apart: For the Residential Parent

- Do not have expectations that are too high.
- Show your love for your child.
- Don't use your phone as a crutch. Put it down when around your kid.
- Resolve to cope with your emotions and move on with your life.
- Maintain your job, your friendships, and your family relationships.
- Find pleasure in life and pass this on to your child.
- Don't make promises to your child that you cannot keep.
- Avoid confrontations with the other parent.
- Expect things to be difficult for a while.
- Stop blaming yourself and focus on the positive things in your life.
- Make your home a place where you are comfortable.
- Plan to be civil to the other parent and to work with him or her to help your child have a better life.

Chapter 6

Communicating with the Other Parent

It is likely that one of the reasons you and the other parent are no longer together is because you have difficulty communicating. You also probably both harbor some negative feelings towards each other. Despite all of this, you must develop a way to talk to each other so that your child can receive the benefits of having two parents. Even if you have a detailed, court-ordered parenting plan, problems and conflicts are going to arise that will require communication. Finding a way to communicate will certainly not be easy, but it will make your contact with each other easier and it will reduce stress for everyone involved.

Try to Develop a New Relationship

You and the other parent are going to be parents together for the rest of your lives. Even though you are divorced or not together anymore, the parenting part of your relationship continues. It is a fact you cannot change and a bond you cannot break. Try to sit down and talk to each other simply as parents, not as two people whose marriage or relationship went bad. If you can both agree that you each want what is best for your child, then you can find a way to achieve it together. Resolve to be co-parents. Agree not to argue about past events and to talk only about the foreseeable future. It takes a lot of work and a lot of effort to develop a new parenting relationship with each other, but it is possible.

It is easy to fall back into your old patterns of arguing, baiting, disagreeing, or trying to hurt each other. Agree that you will try not to let this happen. Think about how important your child is to you. You cannot change who your child's other parent is, no matter how much you might want to. You also cannot change how the other parent behaves. You can only focus on finding a way to cooperate with him or her to make life better for your child.

You both know you've got to parent together, but if you can actually verbalize this to each other it can go a long way towards making you really committed to it. Tell the other parent that your goal is to respect him or her and help your child continue to have a meaningful relationship with him or her. There may be all kinds of bad feelings between you and the other parent, but if you can just tell him or her that you will try to work together, you will have offered an olive branch that will help you parent together effectively. This might not be the easiest or most comfortable thing to do, and that is ok. Making the effort is what is important.

You are both human and will both slip up. Accept that you will both break the rules once in a while but try to get past the mistakes and focus on keeping your child's welfare your priority. Remind yourself constantly that you are doing this for your child. Make a fresh start and try to have a parenting relationship that is separate from your own personal relationship.

Set Co-Parenting Rules for Yourselves

If you and the other parent are going to co-parent with as little drama as possible, you need to set up some basic rules you will both follow. The following are some examples of rules that will help both of you cope (but you should create some personalized rules that work for your situation).

- Schedule changes must be requested as soon as possible and preferably no later than 24 hours in advance.

- Vacation travel dates must be provided at least one month in advance.
- If the parent picking up or dropping off the child is going to be more than 15 minutes late, he or she will call or text.
- You each will try your best to accommodate schedule changes requested by the other parent.
- You will work together to create rules for your child.
- Decide who will be responsible for washing the clothes worn at the nonresidential parent's home. You may be surprised to learn that this is often one of the most common problems that arises.
- Any items taken to the nonresidential parent's home will be returned with the child (especially crucial items – blankie, jacket, school books, instrument, sports uniforms, sneakers, favorite toy).
- Agree not to argue in front of your child. Whenever an argument starts, develop a word or phrase you will both recognize that will indicate this is something you should discuss later, out of earshot of your child (such as later or table it).
- Your child is not permitted to make changes in the schedule without permission from both of you.
- You will not use your child to transmit messages or money to each other.
- You will contact each other directly, either in person, by phone or text, by email, or in writing.
- You will always check with each other if your child has a complaint about the other parent. Children's perceptions are often skewed and stories tend to grow as they are repeated to other people. Sometimes this is intentional and other times it is not. Always consult the other parent if the child is complaining about something serious before flying off the handle.
- The parent that the child is with at the time is responsible for transporting him or her to scheduled activities, such as sports and classes.
- Decide who will be responsible for your child's meal if transfer time is scheduled near a normal meal time.
- The parent who is with the child is the one responsible for taking the child to the doctor for sick visits.

Think about what other ground rules you will need to have in place to facilitate sharing parenting time and add any that are helpful to your specific situation. You probably know the other parent's hot spots and he or she probably knows yours. Try to avoid setting each other off and make some rules that can help you both.

Be Flexible

Flexibility is a must in making a parenting plan work. Think of a parenting plan as a give and take situation, not as giving in, letting the other parent win, or being victorious. If you let the other parent change weekends with you this time, then when you ask for a change, it shouldn't be a problem. This might mean you and the other parent will have to acknowledge and accept that you both have separate lives now, and that won't be easy.

This does not mean you should make changes on a regular basis. Your child needs stability. But some changes are okay. Don't feel that just because the judge told you to begin visitation at 5:30 p.m. on Wednesdays that it is written in stone. You and the other parent can make any adjustments to the schedule as long as you both agree to do so (and courts WANT you to do this, instead of coming back and clogging up the calendar to ask them to make such a small change). If 6:00 p.m. works better for both of you, then make that your scheduled time. Be prepared to have to make adjustments as your life, the other parent's life, and your child's life change and grow. Parenting plans need to develop as situations do.

Develop a Written Schedule Together

Even if you have a court-ordered schedule, you should still put it on a calendar so you both have a written schedule of where your child will be when. A shared online calendar is the easiest way to do this. Plan out the schedule for the whole year, but know that that is subject to change. Then look at it and talk about what needs to be changed. If you have to go out of town when your child is supposed to be with you or if the other parent wants a weekend alone to prepare for an exam, make adjustments. Look at how the holidays will be divided and talk about whether or not they will work the way they are currently scheduled and make adjustments as needed. Plan out any vacations either of you will be taking with the child at this time as well if possible. Remember to be flexible, reasonable, and calm. Treat this the same way you would treat any other scheduling situation in your everyday life. If you feel you're starting to get upset, pretend you are at the dentist just trying to schedule your next cleaning. Treat this in the same no-drama way if possible.

Bite Your Tongue

The most important thing to remember when dealing with the other parent is to think before you speak. This can be hard to do, but it's worth the effort. Try not to have knee-jerk responses to the things about him or her that irritate you. Try not to get angry or upset in front of the other parent. Go home and punch your pillow or scream in the shower afterwards, but do not get into confrontations. This does not mean you have to be a victim or give in on every point. Choose your battles carefully and try to minimize them. Be polite and courteous to the other parent even if you do not get the same treatment in return. It is very hard for a situation to blow up into a giant war if one person is completely calm. Keep in mind that you are putting up with it all for the benefit of your child.

Divide Responsibilities

If the other parent was always the one to take your child for haircuts, maybe you want that to continue. Perhaps you were the parent who handled all doctor appointments. It's a good idea to talk about these kinds of responsibilities and develop a plan for who will handle them. If not, you may make an appointment for your child's dental check-up only to find the other parent made one as well. Decide who is going to be primarily in charge of: haircuts; medical, dental, vision, and orthodontia check-ups (you may decide sick visits will be handled by whomever is with the child when he or she becomes ill or injured); and, purchasing seasonal or once-a-year items like new shoes, boots, coats, school and camp supplies, and sports equipment.

Many parents agree to let the residential parent handle these things, but involving the other parent will allow your child to feel as if both parents are involved in his or her life.

It's also a good idea to be clear about who is going to be in charge of correspondence with the school and activities. If a permission slip comes home with your child and the other parent signs it but the event is happening during your scheduled time, you're suddenly out of the loop. It may be a good idea to designate one parent to handle these and to be certain that everything involving your child goes on your shared calendar so it's there for everyone to see.

Arguments

Never, ever argue in front of your child if you can help it. Your child is already struggling to believe that the divorce or breakup is not his or her fault. When parents argue about the parenting, all the child thinks is that the parents are arguing because of the child. Handle all disagreements when your child is not around. It's not easy to put a cork in an argument and you will not always be successful, but if you try it will help your child feel more comfortable.

Setting Up Times to Talk

Some parents find that they are best able to communicate with each other if they schedule a weekly or monthly meeting or phone call to discuss their child. Do so when you can talk without your child overhearing. Talk about problems that have come up, schedule changes that need to be made, reactions your child is having and things coming up in the future. Speak calmly and rationally as best you can, pushing aside all of those emotions that will get in the way of your objective. Keep in mind that texts are great for quick schedule changes, but don't take the place of talking when there are real issues at hand, such as concerns over how your kid is doing at school or discussions about changing the overall schedule.

If child support needs to be discussed, do so either at the end of the meeting or at an entirely different time. It can be helpful to keep money and parenting completely separate so that frustrations about money don't leak over into your parenting interactions. It can be helpful to think of wearing a different hat for each of those discussions so that your demeanor is completely different.

The need for such formal meetings will dissipate the longer you are divorced, and you will eventually learn to have quick unscheduled phone calls or chats. There may be times when large problems develop in the future, and you might find that resuming a regular meeting or phone call schedule can help.

Getting Help

If you are having trouble communicating with each other (after all, old habits are hard to break), consider seeing a mediator who can help you work through the issues and develop a new way to talk to each other without arguments. It really is possible to do so and you may be surprised at how well the mediation process works. Mediation not only helps you solve your current problem, but teaches you conflict resolution skills you can use in the future.

When All Else Fails: Try the Business Transaction Approach

If you have tried working together, if you have tried biting your tongue and none of it has worked, if you and the other parent are at each other's throats and cannot agree on anything, think of your dealings with the other parent as a business transaction. Be polite, but do not argue or display emotion if you can help it. Communicate by written notes or email if you cannot talk. You want to accomplish the task of parenting together and exchanging your child. Remember that this is not about you, your feelings, or the way you deserve to be treated. This is about making sure your child has two parents. Treat the situation as one you just need to deal with, as you would treat any other kind of activity in your daily life.

Parenting Together Apart: For the Residential Parent

You might have a cranky cashier at the grocery store, and while his or her behavior is not appropriate or polite, you somehow find a way to deal with it so you can get your groceries. View parenting in the same light. You have a goal you want to accomplish (making sure your child has relationships with two parents) and the way to accomplish it is to keep your feelings to yourself and just get through the situation. Arranging and facilitating regular parenting time is part of your responsibilities as the residential parent, so take whatever steps you need to be able to work out plans with the other parent. Keep reminding yourself that you are doing this for your child. It will not be easy, but if you have the goal of a well-adjusted child in mind, you will have more motivation.

When It is Unbearable

Sometimes, you and the other parent might get to the point where you absolutely despise each other and the thought of being polite to him or her may make you cringe. If you feel that you and the other parent simply cannot communicate at all at this point, you probably need a break from each other. Have your child ready for scheduled visits, deal with the transfer and simply do not talk to the other parent beyond the essentials. If you can't even handle this, then ask a friend or relative to help you with the transfers. Let your best friend or sister open the door and make sure all of the child's belongings go with the child. If you need to avoid contact for a while, it's okay. It will probably ease the tension if you avoid each other for a while and let things cool off. Ignore texts or calls from the other parent if they are not urgent. It takes a while for emotions to simmer down after a divorce or separation. Most likely, things will eventually improve to the point where you can exchange your child without too much discomfort. But this may take time and you need to patient. Although you might want to, you can't decide you want to cancel all parenting exchanges because it is too uncomfortable for you. It's important for your child. Even if your child does not seem to have a very good relationship with the other parent right now, you have to give them the opportunity to know each other and be together.

Developing a good parenting partnership can take time. You can't go directly from the heat of a nasty custody battle to cooperating fully with each other the next day. This is something you will gradually build up to. Take baby steps if necessary. Be patient.

PARENTING COMMUNICATION RULES

- **Don't raise your voice or yell.** The best way to communicate with the other parent is by using a neutral, calm voice. Raising your voice will lead to an argument. Even if the other person yells, keep your voice at a normal level because it will deescalate the conflict.
- **Be clear about what you are talking about.** Try to address only one issue at a time. Don't confuse things by bringing up other topics or problems.
- **Let the past go.** Don't try to discuss what has happened in the past with your relationship. Focus on the present, your parenting relationship, and the future with regard to your child.
- **Repeat yourself if necessary.** Sometimes you may try to discuss an issue relating to parenting and the other parent will try to bring up other things. If you respond, you will both be diverted from the important issue at hand – the parenting topics. Repeat your question or wait calmly until he or she answers it.
- **Choose your times.** If you want to have a real discussion with the other parent, do so at a time when you are both able to talk freely and are not rushed or tired.
- **Try to talk in "I" phrases instead of "you" phrases.** If you are having a problem with visitation, say things like, "I'm having trouble picking Trevor up at 4 p.m. Could we change it to 5 p.m.?" Avoid saying things like, "You are going to have to change the time we exchange Trevor." Try to focus the sentence on your needs, your problem, your situation, and avoid sentences that sound like accusations, criticisms, or complaints.

- **Don't discuss things you don't need to.** This means letting some things go and focusing on the important issues. Choose your issues and let the smaller ones go.
- **Speak with respect.** Remember, this is your child's other parent and is extremely important to your child. This is the person you created life with and/or raised a child with. He or she deserves to be treated with respect, even if you believe that he or she is truly not worthy of it.

Chapter 7

Encouraging and Assisting with Visitation

You may feel that, in many ways, your hard work is done. You survived the separation or divorce, and negotiated the court system so that your child would live primarily with you. You take the time to make sure you have a good relationship with your child and anything the other parent does or does not do isn't your problem at this point.

Actually, this is not quite the case. You do need to be involved with your ex's parenting time and your child's relationship with the other parent to make sure that your child is able to handle it and get the benefits from it.

You may feel that you are the parent who is most responsible for your child and that you are the one who is best suited to care for your child (which is why you were awarded residential custody). If this is the case, then part of your responsibility to make sure your child maintains a healthy relationship with the other parent. If you felt that your child was not maintaining a healthy relationship with a grandparent or a friend, you would probably make some effort to improve it. Part of parenting after divorce or separation is supporting and encouraging the relationship with the other parent.

If you feel that the other parent is a reasonably good parent, and it is important to you that you share responsibility for your child, then it is equally important that you encourage your child to see the other parent and spend time with him or her. If you feel the other parent is not the greatest parent, it is even more important that you support and encourage their time together, since he or she may not be completely on top of it. Your child lives with you most of the time, and part of your responsibility as a residential parent is making sure that your kid continues to have a second parent and benefit from that relationship.

Your Feelings about Time with the Other Parent

The one thing to remember when communicating with your child, verbally and nonverbally, is to be positive and encouraging about the time he or she spends with the other parent. While controlling the words that come out of your mouth is definitely doable, it can be more difficult to stop yourself from displaying your resentment, anger, or hurt in nonverbal ways. After all, your feelings are real and it's very hard not to let them show. Remember that your actions convey as much information as your words. If you slam the door when the other parent leaves, speak to him or her in a hostile voice in front of your child, or allow your body language to convey your anger, this information will get through to your child and inform him or her that you really wish he or she wasn't spending time with the other parent. This is hurtful and confusing to children and teens alike. While it's impossible to suppress all of your feelings, try to take a calm and reserved approach around your child. Your child picks up on your emotional cues so trying to be neutral about the time with the other parent is the best bet.

THINGS TO SAY TO YOUR CHILD ABOUT VISITATION
- It's important to me that you spend time with Mom/Dad.
- I want you to spend time with Mom/Dad because she/he is your other parent and that will never change.
- Yes, I'll miss you, but I'm glad you'll have some time with Mom/Dad.

- Have fun! See you when you come home.
- I'm sorry you don't feel like going, but today is your day to be with Mom/Dad and you have to go.
- He/she will always be your Dad/Mom and I wouldn't have it any other way.

THINGS NOT TO SAY TO YOUR CHILD ABOUT VISITATION
- I wish I could go, too.
- Well, I guess you'll just have to miss the big family reunion at the beach, since you'll be with Mom/Dad. Too bad.
- You'd rather be with him/her anyhow, so just go.
- Wouldn't you rather just stay here with me and watch a movie?
- I am so nervous when you are alone with him/her.
- I don't know why you want to go with him/her.
- You always come home in a bad mood. He/she is such a bad influence.

Your Responsibility for Parenting Time

When the court gave you residential custody of your child, the judge also gave you the responsibility for making sure your child continues to see the other parent and have the other parent in his or her life. In fact, if you interfere with or try to prevent time with the other parent, this can be the legal basis for a change of custody (it's called custodial interference). As tempting as it is, you can't just wipe your hands and walk away saying to the other parent, "You're on your own. Good luck." You have a responsibility to make sure that time with the other parent is a priority in your child's life. Don't schedule your child for a regular activity on the other parent's days without discussing it with him or her or seeing what arrangements can be made. Make sure you emphasize to your child that time with the other parent is important and something that must be given priority in his or her life.

If your child is playing with friends and doesn't want to go spend time with the other parent and you say ok and cancel, it's on you. You're the parent. You're the one who is supposed to get the kid out the door. No matter what your child wants, you're supposed to make sure your child has time with the other parent.

Kids Who Don't Want to Go

Sometimes children act as if they do not want to go with the other parent. Don't panic if this happens because it's very common; in fact almost every child will refuse to go at one point or another. Your job is to make sure your child does go though. It can be really hard to make a child who is crying or throwing a fit about the other parent go and spend time with him or her. One of the best ways to handle this is to treat it like an obligation that belongs to the child, not something that you personally are deciding. For example, your child might not want to get out of bed and go to school some days, but you make him because it's his responsibility to go to school. Likewise, the judge has set up this parenting plan and your child has to follow it. It's not up to you to change it. In fact, present it as if you have no power or influence over it all, the same as with school.

Following the parenting plan is not optional for your child, just as it is not optional for you. When your children are adults, they can decide for themselves if they wish to continue their relationships with their parents. While they are children they do not have this choice. You are the parent and you must make sure that your child follows the rules that have been created for your family. Furthermore, you have been ordered by the court to allow parenting time at scheduled times. If you do not, you are violating a court order and can be held in contempt of court, which can mean jail time and fines, not to mention the fact that you could lose custody. When the day comes when your child refuses to go (and it probably will happen), you are responsible for making him or her go. If you do not, you are giving in and you're also making it clear to the other parent that you don't think his or her parenting time is important. Be absolutely clear with your child that there is no arguing and no way to change this.

It is important that you and the other parent present a united front on this matter. You must both act as if the scheduled time is going to happen and you must not give in. If you give in and allow your child to stay home with you once, it becomes clear to the child that he or she can play one of you off the other, that you don't mean what you say, and that you are not serious about how important time with the other parent is. It also makes the other parent feel as if you are not working with him or her and are trying to undercut him or her and find ways out of the schedule you both agreed to (even if that's not your intent, and usually it's not. Usually the residential parent feels like he or she is trying to do what's best for the child, but cancelling parenting is not what's best for you child). In short, giving in will negatively affect all of you. And keep in mind that if YOU give in and let your child stay home, the other parent then might feel empowered to let the child stay at his or her house when your child is supposed to come home to you.

If you think that you somehow win by keeping your child home, you are mistaken. You're not proving the other parent is a bad or inadequate parent. What you're doing is telling your child that you don't think the relationship with the other parent is important. You're helping your child push away the other parent. You are effectively denying your child his or her right to have two parents that love and care for him or her, through good times and bad times.

Sometimes there are good reasons why a child doesn't want to go with the other parent. Ask your child why he or she doesn't want to go. Often, it will be because he or she is just engaged in something that seems more fun at your house. However, there may be things about the time at the other house your child doesn't like. It isn't a good idea for you to get involved in this and try to argue with the other parent about it. Your child has a relationship with the other parent and the two of them are going to have to figure it out on their own. You can suggest that your child discuss his or her concerns with the other parent, and you can also help your kid think about the best way to phrase things, but you just can't get in the middle of this. Your child and the other parent must work out their relationship on their own. You're no longer in the middle of this. And honestly, that can actually be of some relief if you've spent years as the mediator. It's not your job to make the relationship work, but it is your responsibility to make sure the relationship has time to work. That's an important distinction.

When Your Child Would Rather Be There

Just as there are times when your child will refuse to go with the other parent, there will be times when he or she will not want to come home or will make noise about preferring to be with the other parent. All of this is normal and will most likely happen at some point in your family. Of course it's going to hurt your feelings. Your feelings would have been hurt before the divorce or separation if your child had refused to spend time with you then. Don't let it get to you.

Remember that children rebel, and it is natural and normal. Stick to your guns and to your schedule. Children don't get to choose where they live and which parent they would rather be with. You and the other parent must make sure your child understands that you both will always listen to what he or she has to say, but that the parents are the ones who make the decisions about living arrangements.

Your time with your child is just as important as the other parent's time with your child and it's important that you support each other and stand by the schedule.

All that being said, there are circumstances where a change of custody could be the best thing for a child. It is common for teens to have a real need to spend more time with the parent of the same sex. Should it become clear that your older child truly wants and needs to live with the other parent, you, the other parent, and the child need to discuss this, and you may need to talk to your lawyer. It may be a good idea to talk with a family therapist or counselor to find out if this is really what is best for your child. It would be up to the other parent to file court papers seeking a change in custody at this point.

Dealing with Transitions

For most children, the transition from one parent to another is the most difficult part of parenting time. When your child goes from one parent to the other, expect there to be some difficulties. To make transitions easier when your child is returned to you, talk with your child about what you have planned and what you will be doing that day. When the child is going to the other parent, talk about what he or she will be doing with the other parent and when he or she will see you next. Whatever you do, don't make transition time a time of wishy-washy flip flopping decisions. Changing your mind about whether or not you will send your child lets him or her know plans are not completely set and opens the door for your child to try to influence the decision with whining, begging, or refusals.

Many parents find that the most difficult part of time with their children is the time at the beginning and end of their scheduled time. It's hard for children to leave one parent and instantly get into the groove with the other. When your child comes home, give each other a little space to adjust without immediately jumping into an intense activity together. Allow your child time to unpack or get a snack if you are at home or time to adjust to the surroundings if you are in public. Younger kids may benefit from being distracted with toys or activities. Once your child becomes interested in something, the focus shifts and the situation calms down. Even with older kids, at some point you have to stop letting the situation be about how miserable your kid is and make it about something else. Distractions can be good for everyone.

Teens also have problems transitioning and may be moody, silent, or hostile. Keep in mind that teens may just be moody, silent, or hostile on any given day and it might have nothing to do with the transition at all! Give your teen space when he needs it.

To ease the transition back to the other parent, tell your young child in advance when he or she will go with the other parent and give some additional reminders, such as two hours before, one hour before and half an hour before. Make sure when you part that you are able to point to the next time you will be together or the next time you will text or call, and make some reference to what you will be doing together then. Also point out if you will have phone or email contact before then.

Whether you should reach out to the other parent to help with transitions is something you need to use trial and error for. If your child is being whiny or difficult about being at your house, a call from the other parent could calm things down or ratchet things up. Try it and see what happens and determine if it is useful. The same is true when your child goes with the other parent. Having you call or text could help or could just make it worse. Communicate with the other parent before getting involved. That being said, anytime your child reaches out to you, you should respond. But loop the other parent in on what's going on.

TIPS TO REDUCE TRANSITIONING ISSUES
- Transition in a public place if necessary.
- Use school beginning or ending as a transition time so the child does not go directly from one parent to the other.
- Transition at a neutral place, such as a relative's home if doing so at your homes is not working.
- Don't shoehorn your child from one parent's car to the other's. Spend a moment or two somewhere before popping him or her back in a car if possible.
- Tell your child a joke or a funny story or do something to lighten the mood.
- Remind your child when you will be together again, or if it is the beginning of your time, remind him or her when he or she will be with the other parent next.
- Give your child some space to adjust. Allow some quiet individual time if you are at home before getting into an activity together.
- Keep your thoughts or complaints about the other parent under wraps.

- Don't try to use transition time as a time to discuss big issues with your child.
- Be polite and friendly to the other parent. Smile!
- Try not to rush. Being frantic just makes things worse.
- If hugging and kissing is natural for you, do it: If it isn't, don't.
- Make it clear you are happy to see your child when your time together begins.
- Don't act sad or upset when your child is leaving you. It's normal to feel this way, but don't burden your child with this.
- Don't try to get your child to hide or suppress feelings of sadness or anger. Work on helping him or her through it.
- Use distraction to get your child thinking about something else.
- Don't use transition time as negotiation time with the other parent. Keep the mood cooperative, if at all possible.

Some parents find that transitions can be eased if the parent the child is currently with transports the child to the other parent. So, the other parent would bring the child home to you and you would take the child to the other parent's house. Transitioning in a public place, such as a park, a mall, or a restaurant, can make things easier. It may also be easier if you do not transition directly with the other parent. He or she could pick your child up at school and return him or her there the next school morning. In some situations, a child may do better with transitions if another adult is involved. For example, the child could be dropped off and picked up at a grand-parent's house.

When the Other Parent Is a Crappy Parent

While it's not often that both parents agree about everything after a divorce, most parents at least feel somewhat comfortable leaving their child with the other parent. If your situation is different and you truly know the other parent is simply a terrible parent, you need to come up with some strategies for coping because you are required to follow your court order (at least until you can get it changed—talk to your lawyer about that).

If your child is old enough to use a phone, make sure he or she knows to call you at any time if he/she is scared, afraid, confused, left alone, lost, hurt, or in any kind of distress. Develop a strategy of regularly texting your child to touch base so that you know everything is okay.

If your child is too young for a phone, you're going to need a support system. Get your friends and family to be there for you so you can call or text any time to express your worries and talk you down. If you are truly deeply concerned, you could introduce yourself to the other parents' neighbors and give them your number to call if they ever have any concerns. Be aware however this will likely get back to your ex and could make things more difficult.

Remember that most likely your child will okay and the judge made this call and you have to follow it. You're doing everything you can to keep your kid safe and happy. Breathe. Stay calm.

If you need to, it's ok to drive by where your child will be to see for yourself everything is ok. Try not to do this a lot, or to be seen, but if you truly are worried this can let you see with your own eyes.

Helping Your Child with Long-Distance Parenting

If the other parent lives far away, you need to develop some strategies for helping your child cope with long-distance situation.

Even though your child is physically separated from the other parent, this does not mean they have to be out of touch or emotionally separated. Encourage your child and the other parent to share regular phone calls, texts, IMs, emails, Skype calls, and more. Encourage them to send each other letters and packages. Take photos your child can send to the other parent. Send copies of report cards and videos. If your child is into gaming, see if there are games they could play together.

When the other parent and your child do see each other in person, it will be need to be in bigger chunks of time than the typical schedule. If your child is very young, it makes more sense for the other parent to come to your area so that the child can continue to have time with both parents. As a child grows, he or she will be able to visit the other parent out of town. Think about how you will arrange transportation. Perhaps you could drive the child there and the other parent could drive the child home. Some parents are comfortable allowing their children to fly alone and airlines can make accommodations for this so that an employee will escort the child (most airlines allow this beginning at age five).

While your child is away with the other parent, make sure that you have frequent phone, text, Skype, and email contact so that the child knows you are still accessible.

Vacations

When your child vacations with you or with the other parent, it is important that you and the other parent share itineraries with each other. Children should be able to have virtual contact with the parent they are away from throughout the trip, as desired. Don't be surprised if your child goes away with your ex and you get one text then never hear another peep! It's a sign your child is busy and happy. Check in with the other parent if you are worried.

Coping with All that Stuff

One of the main things divorced parents argue about is their child's belongings. "You didn't send any clean underwear," "How could you forget to bring his soccer uniform back?" or "What do you mean you can't find the pacifier?" Dealing with your child's stuff is one of the biggest difficulties you may have to cope with.

It's a good idea to set some ground rules about the belongings. There are some items that will need to travel with the child, such as school books, instruments, sports equipment, special toys, blankies, coats, cell phone, tablet or laptop, and shoes. It is best if the other parent is encouraged to provide some items that can stay at his or her home. He or she can purchase some clothes, toys, books, and so on to keep at his or her home, or maybe there are some items you are willing to send from your home that can stay at the other home. This will reduce the amount of items being exchanged.

Laundry is a heated point of contention with some parents. The best policy is to return the clothes that belong at the other house laundered, if there is time. Discuss this with the other parent. Older children can take on this responsibility themselves.

Develop a system for making sure the right items go with your child to the other house. It may be helpful to post a list on your refrigerator or bulletin board so that nothing is forgotten while packing. In the beginning you will need to assist with packing. It will take a while for your child to get into the swing of it. Children over age eight should be encouraged to eventually manage their own belongings.

If your child returns home and essential items are missing, you will need to contact the other parent and arrange for him or her to drop them off or for you to go pick them up. Encourage the other parent to use a list to keep track of what needs to come home. You can also send a checklist of everything you have packed if you think this will help. You may wish to send a list by email that be saved on the parent's phone and always be accessible.

SAMPLE LIST OF BELONGINGS THAT TRAVEL WITH YOUR CHILD
Infant or Toddler
- snowsuit/coat
- clothes
- blanket
- pacifier
- special toys
- medication
- any bottles, cups, or dishes that came with the child
- diaper bag

School-Age Child
- backpack
- homework
- books
- sneakers
- clothes
- sports uniform/equipment
- tablet, laptop, or phone
- charger cords and headphones
- assignment notebook
- stuffed animals, action figures, or toys
- musical instrument
- favorite pillow
- lunchbox
- coat
- boots/shoes
- medication

Teen
- cosmetics and other hygiene items that he or she is particular about
- hair brush/comb
- homework and school books
- backpack
- coat
- uniform and sports equipment
- diary or journal
- boots/shoes
- bag of clothes and accessories
- cell phone
- medication
- musical instrument
- laptop, tablet, and/or phone

- Charger cords and headphones
- wallet or purse
- school ID

Medication

Always send instructions if you are sending medication with your child and ask that the other parent keep track of when doses are given. It may be helpful to download a dosage app chart for both of you to use. Ask him or her to record all prescription and non-prescription medications that are given. Explain that it is important for you to know when medicine was given so that you can give the next dose on time. In return, you must let the other parent know when you last gave medication, so he or she can determine when to give the next dose. If you have a chronically ill child, it is a good idea to have the other parent talk to the doctor at some point to review medications and treatment.

Chapter 8

Dealing with Schedules

One of the hardest things to deal with once you are divorced or separated is learning to live with the parenting schedule. Parenting on a schedule is a learned skill. You're used to your child being at home whenever you are and being free to go anywhere when you go. Parenting was something that happened organically. Things are different now, and although your child is the one who is going to be spending time with the other parent, you are the one who has to make this schedule a part of both your lives.

The Schedule

Most families have a schedule that is set by the court or agreed to by both parents. This schedule can be adjusted if both you and the other parent agree to alter it (and courts encourage you to do this—they don't want you coming back to take up the court's time to make adjustments to pick up times or swapping weekends). Once the schedule is set, it is important that both you, the other parent, and your child have it on a calendar. A shared electronic calendar is the best way to make sure everyone is on the same page. There is nothing worse than forgetting to have your child ready for pick up or forgetting to be home on time for your child's return because you got your days mixed up. If you have trouble staying on top of things, set up automatic reminders to be sent to your phone.

You also need to help your child learn to live by the schedule For young children, a color-coded hard copy calendar is very helpful. Color one parent's days blue and the other's red (or any other color you choose) and on the transition days, split the day in half with a color on each side. This visual aid will assist younger children in seeing where they will be on each day and will help prepare them for the transitions. Elementary age kids will do well with a traditional wall calendar. Teens are more likely to be comfortable with a digital calendar.

When you create a schedule, it is a good idea to have some basic schedule rules in place, such as whoever is with the child at 6:00 p.m. will feed him or her dinner, or whoever is with the child until 8:00 will assist with homework. These basic rules will allow you to avoid having discussions and negotiations about these basic daily events.

SAMPLE SCHEDULING RULES

- Changes to the schedule require 24 hours notice, except in emergencies.
- The parents will try to accommodate reasonable schedule change requests made by each other.
- If the parent providing transportation will be late, he or she will call as soon as possible to let the other parent and child know.
- Each parent will be assigned pick-up and drop-off duties that will remain the same. Pick-ups and drop-offs will be at a set time. For example, Parent A will always drop off the child at 7:00 p.m. every other Friday, and Parent B will always drop off the child at 2:00 p.m. every other Sunday. These times will not change unless the parents agree.
- The parents will meet, talk, or communicate once a month to exchange scheduling information.

- The nonresidential parent will contact the school and extracurricular activities leaders for copies of calendars and schedules. If a calendar change notice is sent home with the child, it will be shared with the nonresidential parent.
- Schedule change requests will be made directly by one parent to the other and messages will not be carried by the child.
- If the child has a scheduled activity planned during parenting time, the parent who is with the child will transport the child (if needed) to and from the activity.
- The nonresidential parent shall have the right to have the child skip a normally planned activity scheduled during his or her visitation time if he or she has a more important, one-time event planned (for example a family reunion would trump a baseball practice).
- Each parent will maintain a calendar and keep track of parenting times and the child's activities.
- An age appropriate calendar will be maintained for the child's use.

Understanding Your Child's Schedule

Remember that your child has a schedule of his or her own. Many children and teens (see Chapters 4 and 13 for more information about teens) participate in after school activities and have various lessons and classes to attend. Obtain copies of all correspondence that deals with your child's schedule. Make sure these notices do not get left in your child's backpack or bag if they are sent as hard copy. It is also important that the other parent be familiar with your child's schedule. Suggest that the other parent request that the school coach, group leader, and so on copy him or her on all correspondence, whether it is in print or by email.

The school calendar should be available on the school's web site. It's also important to remember that sometimes school information is sent home with the child. You and the other parent should to agree that whoever receives this information should share it with the other parent. Each parent is responsible for getting his or her name added to email notification lists.

Mark school events and all scheduled activities on the shared calendar, so everyone can stay on top of what's happening when.

Dealing with Conflicts

Many parents feel torn when faced with a conflict between parenting time and a child's scheduled activity. Think about these situations in this way. When all of you lived together in one home, did your child have to skip the prom or a soccer game because one of you wanted to spend time with him or her?

Probably not. You or your spouse took the child to the event (or saw him or her before and afterwards) and fit in family time around it. This is how life should continue. Continue to allow your child to participate in activities that are important to him or her. If you or the other parent constantly require a child to skip activities, all you will get out of it will be resentment. If your child has an event planned on the same night he or she is supposed to spend the evening with the other parent, see if it can be arranged for the other parent to take the child to and from the activity and fit in some family time before or after it.

The same goes for your time with your child. Do the best you can to get your child to his or her scheduled events. You should never, ever place your child in the position of having to choose between spending time with a parent and an activity that is important to him or her. There will be times when there are conflicts and you will have to make a decision at that time about where the child will go, but remember that this is a decision for the parents to make and not the child. Children should not be asked to choose between their parents and their friends or activities.

If you find that there are too many ongoing conflicts with scheduled parenting time, then you and the other parent should try to rearrange the schedule to take into consideration the child's schedule.

When to Say No
Although it is important for your child to continue in sports and activities that are fun and enriching, there does come a time when you should say no. If your child is scheduled for something every single day (or several things a day), it might be time to think about cutting back. It's also important to take into consideration the driving time between houses. If the other parent lives 45 minutes away, it's not going to be reasonable for him to pick your kid up from school, go home, drive back for a basketball game, then drive home. Something's got to give. You don't want your kid to spend half her life in the car. You might need to rearrange the parenting schedule so that less time is spent driving back and forth.

If you and your child or the other parent and the child have something important planned (such as a camping trip together or your grandmother's 90'h birthday party) that conflicts with a planned activity, you are using your authority as a parent when you decide the child will have to miss the activity just once. Be sure to explain this calmly to your child. The other parent might have something important planned together that might necessitate missing one of the child's activities sometime as well.

Your Child's Friends
When kids reach elementary school, friends become extremely important. Encourage your child to invite friends to your home. Suggest that the other parent invite some of the child's friends over once in a while. Continuing to see friends at both homes will help your child adjust to the new life and help him or her maintain the friendships that are so important. It will be up to the other parent to agree to this—it's not your job to plan these get-togethers. Tell your child to discuss this with the other parent. Teens are another story entirely. See Chapter 13 for more information about dealing with teens and their friends.

Changing Your Schedule
There may come a time when you find that you do not have enough time with your child. Perhaps you are working a strange schedule or your child is with

the other parent on all of your free days. Part of being a parent is spending time with your child. If you find that this is not happening, maybe some changes need to be made. Talk to the other parent about changing when parenting time takes place. Look at your child's schedule to see if perhaps he or she could change some activities around. Don't forget to take a good, hard look at your own schedule. Maybe you can get a different work or class schedule. Perhaps you could adjust when you see your own friends. Your child is a central part of your life and it is important that your schedule reflects this.

If you find that, because of the way the child's schedule and the other parent's schedule are arranged, they are not seeing as much of each other as they should, talk to the other parent. Ask if he or she has noticed this. Perhaps he or she could make some changes to his or her schedule. You can't force him or her to do this, but you can show that it is important to you that your child has enough time with the other parent. Remember that changes to the parenting schedule can only be made if both you and the other parent agree to them.

Equal Time Problems

You have a set schedule you are supposed to follow. Look at your schedule and figure out approximately how many days or hours the schedule gives the other parent with your child in a week or in a month. If changes are made to the schedule, he or she should still end up with roughly the same amount of time per month. If the other parent's time is normally scheduled from 7:00 p.m. on Friday to 2:00 p.m. on Sunday, and an alteration is made so your child doesn't go until 9:00 p.m. on Friday, then technically you should change the Sunday time to 4:00 p.m. or add some time later in the month.

This can get very nit-picky if you or the other parent try to be militant about it. Try to make sure the other parent is getting roughly the same amount of time each month. A few hours here or there aren't going to make a huge difference, but if he or she is losing a lot of time on a consistent basis, he or she may become angry about it or feel cheated. Additionally, you need to remember that this time really belongs to your child, so he or she is the one being cheated. You should try to roughly have things work out evenly, but it's important to remember that things will come up for both of you, and you will end up making minor adjustments. Usually, at the end of a year's time these tend to balance each other out.

Solving Confusion about Schedules

Sometimes talking about schedules can get confusing. If the other parent is supposed to have your child every other weekend, for example, this means that you have the child weekend A, the other parent has the child weekend B, and then it is your turn again weekend C, and so on. If you and the other parent agree to swap weekends, things can get confusing. If the normal schedule of weekends is:

Weekend A: you
Weekend B: the other parent
Weekend C: you
Weekend D: the other parent

and you and the other parent agree that you are going to swap weekends A and B, then the new schedule would be:

Weekend A: the other parent
Weekend B: you
Weekend C: you
Weekend D: the other parent

Don't get confused and think that weekend C should be the other parent's since you are on an alternating schedule. You substituted weekend B for weekend A, which was your regularly scheduled weekend. Weekend C is your next regularly scheduled weekend. The same applies if the other parent ends up with two weekends in row because of a change.

Another major point of confusion is holidays. If your holiday falls on a weekend or day that is your regularly scheduled time, you will get your

Parenting Together Apart: For the Residential Parent

holiday and regularly scheduled time simultaneously. If it is your holiday and it falls during the other parent's time, you get the time and the other parent does not. Holidays trump regularly scheduled time. There's no make-up for the missed regular time.

If your holiday falls on a weekend or time the child is normally scheduled to be with the other parent, you will get that holiday and you will also have your next regularly scheduled weekend, even if this means you get two weekends in a row. For example:

Weekend A: your regular time
Weekend B: the other parent's regular time, but it is Christmas and it is your turn to have it, so the child will be with you
Weekend C: your regular time
Weekend D: the other parent's regular time

Keep in mind that this can work the other way too—the other parent may end up having the child for two or three weekends some years because a holiday he or she is scheduled to have falls during your regular parenting time.

There can also be confusion if your court-ordered schedule just says you have alternating holidays. You and the other parent need to sit down and work out what these holidays will be. You also want to be sure that you understand if you are alternating the holidays by year, for example:

Christmas last year: your turn
Christmas this year: the other parent's turn
Christmas next year: your turn

Or if you are actually taking an every-other-holiday approach to things, for example:

This Year's Holiday Schedule
New Year's Day: your turn
Easter: the other parent's turn

Memorial Day: your turn
Fourth of July: the other parent's turn
Labor Day: your turn

This continues throughout the year, so that you have one holiday and the other parent gets the next one. This kind of schedule can be hard to follow, especially if your family always celebrates on Christmas Eve and the other parent's family always celebrates on Christmas Day—this kind of schedule could have your child missing both family celebrations. If that happens, work together to tweak it to make it fit everyone's needs. And in fact if your family always does Christmas Eve and the other parent's family always does Christmas Day it would make sense to agree to make those permanent.

Try to avoid these kinds of scheduling confusions by always writing schedules out on a calendar so you can see them and being clear with the other parent about schedule changes. Whatever you do, try not to wait until the last minute to work it out. Family law attorneys are inundated with calls the weeks before Thanksgiving and Christmas from parents who suddenly have a conflict they can't work out. If you're going to need legal intervention you've got to start working on it a few months in advance.

Dealing with Schedule Violations

There will be times when both you and the other parent will make mistakes with regard to the schedule. Try to give each other a break when possible. No one is perfect and mistakes are going to happen. If you find that the other parent consistently makes mistakes about the schedule, first think about what kind of mistakes they are. Do these mistakes actually benefit you? For example, if the parent regularly picks your child up late, this actually gives you more time. You might not want to complain—but you need to remember that again, your child is the one being cheated. However, this can be inconvenient if you have other things planned or other commitments to meet. If this is the case, or if the mistakes happen all the time, then you need to talk to the other parent. Explain that many mistakes are happening and you'd like to make sure that you both have the same dates or times written down. Suggest to the other parent that these mix-ups are confusing, frustrating, or upsetting for your child. Nicely ask if you can all try to stick to the schedule.

If this doesn't work, maybe you could make some permanent changes to the schedule. Perhaps the other parent is consistently late because he or she is getting caught in traffic or is getting out of work late. Changing the time should help eliminate the problem.

You can also try to set some ground rules. For example, if his/her parenting time is supposed to start at 9 a.m. on Saturday, tell the other parent that if he or she does not call in advance to make a schedule change and is not there to pick up the child by 10, then the visit will be forfeited. This is a tough approach, but you are not at the other parent's beck and call. You do have a life and cannot always stay at home all day on the chance that he or she might decide to show up several hours late. Be aware that this will be difficult for your child. You will look like the bad guy. Remember that you will be showing your child that we all have rules, schedules, and deadlines to follow. Do not say negative things about the other parent in front of the child. Simply explain what the rule is and what has happened. If you find that you have a very difficult relationship with the other parent, you may want to document all of this in a journal or on the calendar, so that you cannot be accused of trying to interfere with parenting time.

If none of this works, then you are going to have to tell the other parent that the schedule has to be followed and if he or she refuses to, then you will have to call your attorney. Your attorney may be able to talk to the other parent's attorney and convince him or her to follow it or you may have to go to mediation or to court as a last resort. Keep in mind that nobody can force the other parent to spend time with your child! If he or she does not want to show up, there isn't much you can do about it.

Chapter 9

Holidays

Holidays are a very emotional time for divorced or separated people. They are even more difficult when children are in the equation. Your heart may ache at the thought of being apart from your child during a holiday. Holidays are also difficult for the children. Children are sad and angry that both parents are not there. They are also sure they are hurting the parent they are not with. Try to remember how difficult the situation is for your child and for the other parent. Realize that holidays will always have to be shared in some way from now on and neither parent is going to get to see the child on every holiday. Problems with holidays may pop up again in the future, so refer back to this chapter when needed.

Being Realistic

Whatever great or awful things you expect a holiday to bring, you are probably wrong: Expect it to be good and bad, but not the picture perfect festival or the absolute lonely disaster you are envisioning. Be realistic about your expectations for yourself and your child. View the holiday as another day that may have some nice components or some sad components to it, but don't let it take over your life.

Before a holiday comes around, take some time to talk about it with your child. Discuss whose house he or she will be at, and talk about how you both feel about the plans. Let your child tell you what he or she likes or dislikes about the plan. Think of what you, your child, and the other parent can do to make the holiday go well.

The best way to ensure that a holiday will go well is to think about giving your child the gift of happiness and love. You can give these things to your child no matter where he or she is. Focus on the joy a child deserves to experience, not on the loss or anger you feel. Let your child know that you love him or her and want him or her to have a good holiday, no matter where he or she is each year.

It is also important to understand that you are not solely responsible for your child's happiness. Your child has two parents. You are not required to make the winter holiday season perfect for your child. You should do what feels right to you, but don't think you have to compensate for the other parent. You are also not responsible for helping the other parent manage the holidays. If you were the one who did the shopping when you were together, you're not responsible for making sure the other parent buys appropriate or enough gifts on his or her own. Deal with your own household and let the other parent manage his or hers, unless you really want to be involved in helping the other parent and both of you are comfortable with that.

Holidays with Your Child

When it is your turn to have your child for an important holiday, do not expect it to be of storybook quality. Be prepared for your child to miss the other parent. Discuss what you and your child will be doing and make time to schedule a phone call between your child and the other parent, and possibly the other grandparents. It will be natural for your child to miss the other parent, and a phone call will help make contact again.

Your schedule probably has your child with the appropriate parent on Mother's Day or Father's Day. If you are same sex parents you may alternate each year. Enjoy your day and focus on your relationship with your son or daughter. That's what the holiday is all about, after all. Think of this as a day for celebrating motherhood or fatherhood and all the joys it has brought you. Encourage your child to make a card or gift for the other parent's day and make sure that they see, or at least talk, to each other.

Holidays without Your Child

It is easy to get wrapped up in the pain of spending a holiday alone. It is normal to feel abandoned, left out, and angry when you are unable to spend a holiday with your child. You need to find some way to get yourself through the day.

Be good to yourself that day and do something you normally wouldn't. Feel free to acknowledge your feelings of sadness, anger, loss, and grief Go ahead and wallow, cry, or yell. Your feelings are real and cannot be pushed aside.

TIPS FOR HANDLING HOLIDAYS ALONE
- Spend time with friends or family.
- Attend a religious service if it is part of how you celebrate.
- Donate your time that day to a charity.
- Go to a movie and splurge on popcorn and candy.
- Watch a movie.
- Curl up with a good book.
- Work on a home improvement project.
- Organize your photographs or clean your closets.
- Take a walk.
- Buy yourself a gift.
- Go to a parade, fireworks, or other community event.
- Cook yourself a special holiday meal.

Parenting Together Apart: For the Residential Parent

- Build a dollhouse or racetrack for your child.
- Rearrange the furniture.
- Spend time on Facebook and talk to other parents in the same situation.
- Sleep in and eat breakfast in bed.
- Go away on a trip by yourself
- Get that project done for work that you've been putting off
- Go to a museum.
- Plant a garden.
- Take the time to start a hobby you've never tried.
- Perform a random act of kindness for a stranger.
- Go to the gym.
- Eat junk food.

Next, think about your child. Try to arrange for some phone or Facetime contact on the holiday. Touching base will make you both feel better. It's okay to tell your child how much you miss him or her, but do not make him or her feel sorry for you or guilty. Give your child permission to enjoy the day without you. ("Have a good time at Grandma's house]" or "Have a great time opening those presents!")

If you haven't already done so, schedule an alternate time for you to celebrate the holiday with your child, such as the next day or when the child returns to your home. Remind your child of this during your phone call. Even though it won't technically be the holiday, it can be your holiday. If you and the other parent are alternating holidays, remind yourself and your child that next year you will be together for this holiday.

When you talk to your child or see him or her afterwards, let him or her tell you about how he or she spent the holiday. Try to just listen without criticizing or making judgments. Comments like, "Your grandfather always lets you eat too much candy," will ruin your child's joy in the event. Be positive and let your child know you are happy he or she had a good day. ("I'm glad you got that bicycle you've been wishing for.")

HOLIDAY TRAPS TO AVOID

- **Making plans for every second when you're with your child.** Leave some down time for you and your child to spend together, or for your child to decompress alone.
- **Being overly festive.** Of course you want to make the day special and you want your child to have fun, but too much gaiety can seem false. You also run the risk of making your child feel bad for not being equally thrilled.
- **Emphasizing how lonely and sad you feel if you are away from your kid on the holiday.** The truth is, it stinks, but dwelling on it and trying to elicit guild from your child isn't going to help.
- **Trying to follow the exact same traditions you used to follow as a family.** Nothing can ever truly be as it was and you only bring up bittersweet memories for both of you by trying to recreate the past.
- **Completely reinventing the holiday.** Your child will want some things to be familiar and traditional. Pick some of the things you used to do as a family and incorporate them with some of your own new traditions to make it a special day.
- **Surrounding yourself with too many people.** You don't want your child to get lost in a crowd. Schedule some alone time.
- **Isolating yourselves.** If part of your holiday tradition involves visiting other family members, continue to do so. Focusing all of your time and attention on your child is too much pressure.
- **Doing the "remember when" routine.** A big part of holidays has to do with memories. It's okay to talk about a few things from the past, but in general, try to look forward. Constant reminiscing could easily make you both sad or angry if you dwell on it.
- **Becoming depressed.** It ' natural for both you and your child to feel sad or angry because divorce or separation has changed

your family. It is okay to be honest with your child ("It feels strange to me too not to have Daddy here"), but you should not unload your emotions ("I feel so alone because Mommy doesn't love me anymore"). Acknowledging the changed situation is okay, but dwelling on it is not.

Sharing Holidays

Many families find that in the first few years after a divorce or separation, the children are happiest if they can spend some time with their parents together on holidays. Some families spend part of Christmas morning together or share Thanksgiving dinner. If this is something you would like to do, discuss it with the other parent. You must both be comfortable and willing to make an arrangement like this work. If you do decide to try it, remember to keep things light. An argument will ruin the day.

Sharing holidays is often a good idea in the first year or two after the divorce because it helps ease the transition. Many families transition away from this in later years as children adjust and grow older. If you do share a holiday don't try to make it exactly as it used to be. Things are different now and it's ok to acknowledge that and incorporate that understanding into the plans.

Gifts

Gift-giving can easily turn into a competition between parents for winter holidays and for birthdays. Each tries to give better, more expensive presents to prove he or she is the better parent. The best way to avoid this is to discuss it with the other parent. Some parents agree to discuss any individual items over $100 or $200 with each other before buying it. Other parents give each other ideas about what each is buying so that there is little duplication. Some agree on a total amount each will not exceed. Like everything else involved with parenting, things always work best when there is communication between the parents. Some parents even give some big important gifts together (like a computer, phone, bike, or gaming system). Do whatever works for your situation.

Avoid showering your child with gifts to make up for the time you spend apart. This strategy does not really work. Think about the amount and type of gifts your child received before the divorce. Try to stick to the same plan.

All of this does not mean that you cannot buy your child that computer or puppy he or she has been begging for. If you are purchasing a gift that will be primarily kept or used at your home, it is really your business and not the other parent's. However, think about how you would feel if you got your child a few small gifts and then he or she went to the other parent's house and got a pony. If you're going to be buying an extravagant gift, it might be a good idea to let the other parent know. This might be something you could chip in on together. Even if you buy the gift alone, at least the other parent won't be shocked when he or she learns about it from your child.

Where will your child keep the gifts you give him or her? You should decide ahead of time if you want the item to stay at your home or if your child can decide where to keep it.

Although it is unlikely you and the other parent will exchange gifts, your child certainly will want to give the other parent a gift. You could take your kid shopping or help him shop online for a gift for the other parent or encourage a teen to do so on his own. While you may have bad feelings toward the other parent, remember that your child loves him or her and sharing in the gift-giving will make your child feel happy. If you absolutely are not comfortable helping your child do this, try to see if some other family member can make sure your child has the opportunity to shop for both parents. With preteen or teenaged children, the child can do the shopping if transportation is arranged or they can shop online if they can use your credit card. Teens may need a reminder about getting a gift for the other parent.

Birthdays

You may not see your child on his or her birthday because you and the other parent have agreed to alternate the day or because it falls on a day when the child is with the other parent. Make contact with your child on his or her birthday—a phone call or a quick stop at the front door for a hug. Celebrate at the next opportunity. This is your child's special day. Do not let your problems with the other parent affect it. If the child is with you, make sure he or she has the opportunity to take a call from the other parent. You might want to hint to the other parent that a phone call would help make the day special.

Some parents have a policy of having both parents present at birthday parties. If you and the other parent are both comfortable with this, give it a try. You'll need to coordinate to be sure you don't plan parties for the same time.

You may want to help your child remember the other parent's birthday, just as you might encourage him or her to remember the parent at Christmas.

Solving Holiday Problems

Don't let the holidays derail you. Constant court battles are usually not the answer. Find a way to work things out with the other parent. If you need help dealing with your emotions, see a counselor or therapist. Clergy are also experienced in dealing with holiday emotions and disputes. Do whatever you have to do to get through holidays. Remember that they do come every year, so it is not the end of the world if you have a disappointing experience this year.

Chapter 10

The Single Parent Life

Now that you are through the separation or divorce, it is time for you to look forward. You have a parenting plan that you need to follow and you need to find a way to make it a part of your life and your child's life. You need to move on with your own life, but you also need to make sure you consider your child's needs when you do. You are in a delicate period where you have a lot of decisions to make. You're living alone as a single parent for the first time, and you want to find a way to create a life that will be comfortable for both you and your child. Be aware that there will also be times in the future when you have to readjust your priorities, your plans, and your lifestyle as your child grows older and as different situations develop. (Come back to this chapter then for help.)

Coping with the Changes

Dealing with the divorce or separation and the change in living arrangements was difficult, and it seems like things should get easier now. Things will probably just be different and not really easier. There are going to be bumps along the road as you, your child, and the other parent adjust to the new order of things. There will be times when you are angry that you have to deal with your child alone, times when you will be angry at the other parent for butting in or messing things up, and times when nothing seems like it will ever be right again. All of this is natural and it's important to just you do the best you can under the circumstances. No one is perfect, no one's life is perfect, and no one makes the right decisions all the time. So pick yourself up and move forward, doing the best you can at the time. You're a good parent and a good person, and you can continue on. You can get through the rough times.

Running a House Alone

Here you are, a single parent, with a home and family to manage. This can seem overwhelming if you think about it too much. However, you managed all of these things when you and the other parent were still together, so you can continue to do so now that you are apart. Some things will actually be easier because there won't be any arguing or compromising involved. You can do things your way. Some things will be more difficult as you find yourself learning to do the things around the house that used to be taken care of by the other parent or as you create new ways of doing things. Mostly though, things won't be better or worse—they'll just be different.

The best way to deal with your new reality is to make your own routine, your own rules, and your own plan for living as a single parent. While the thought of suddenly being in charge of the entire household may seem overwhelming, try to take things one at a time. If you sit down and try to face all of your decisions, responsibilities, and changes at once, it is overwhelming. Try coping with one problem or task at a time. Soon you will find that you are getting into a routine and it doesn't seem so frightening. It can also be helpful to make lists. Make a list of everything that needs to be done this week, and then one for everything that needs to be done today. Work on one item on the list at a time. Use a calendar so you can keep track of your commitments, your child's commitments, and the parenting schedule. Above all, remind yourself that you are a competent and resourceful person and if you just take things one day at a time, you will manage fine.

Making Decisions

When you are newly divorced, do not make any radical decisions right away, such as moving, spending a lot of money on household purchases, and so on. Give yourself time to adjust to the new situation. When it's time to make big decisions, you'll know and you will find freedom and joy in making them. Expect changes and decisions to be difficult for your child as well. Certainly, things are going to be topsy-turvy for a while, but everyone in the household will get used to them. You are the parent and you will be making the big decisions. Your child's input should be welcome, but not decisive. Everyone is adjusting, and you and your child have to make some of these adjustments together.

Creating a New Routine

Now is a good time to make small adjustments in your family life. You might decide to do family dinner three nights a week, decide that each child is now responsible for his own laundry, reverse your dining room and your living room, get a cat, or go to a movie as a family once a month. You might decide that just because you and the other parent always did things one way doesn't mean you have to do them that way anymore. Creating new routines can help fill the void of the changes that have happened in your family. It's a chance to infuse some happiness, clear direction, or just some simple change into your household. You have the freedom to change things up as it suits you.

Having a Life

It is important that you continue to have your job, friends, family, and activities. These are the things that make you a well-rounded person and help you cope with stress. Don't give up the things that are important to you.

Parenting is important, but it should not be your entire life. Find a way to balance your needs with those of your child. Continue to be your own person with your own passions and interests. Show your child how important it is to go on living.

Scheduling

Now that a parenting plan is such a big part of your life, it's important to give it priority. You need to get used to living and dying by the schedule. It is especially important in the first few months after a divorce or separation to follow your schedule closely so that your child can adjust to it. It will feel like an imposition to have the schedule infringe upon your new freedom, but remember that you are making sure your child has time with the other parent, which is a reasonable thing to do. The schedule is a tool that helps divide your child's time. It isn't really a cross to bear or a ball and chain. Remember to think of it as your child's time that is being shared. Of course your child wants to share time with both parents and the schedule is a way to help him or her do that. Respect the schedule the same way you respect this sentiment. Some parents feel really tied down and limited by the schedule. Instead of looking at it as something that ties up your time, think of it as something that gives you a little freedom. There are days now when you have no immediate parenting responsibilities and you have the freedom to use that time as you wish. You're not betraying your child if you enjoy this little bit of freedom.

Parenting Alone

If you have a typical parenting plan, you will be parenting alone for long stretches of time. When you look at the calendar and see stretches of four, five, nine, or twelve days when you will be parenting alone, it may feel overwhelming. But remember you only have to deal with one day at a time. You have been successfully parenting throughout your child's life, and your parenting skills are good—otherwise the court would not have placed you in this situation. Accept that you are not going to be perfect at single parenting. Everyone makes mistakes. Do the best you can at this difficult job.

It can be scary sometimes to feel like you no longer have back up. There are definitely times when having two parents on the scene make things easier, but you'll be happy to find that you can adapt and do just as much yourself.

When you parent alone remember that you have the final say, so try to make decisions and stick to them with your kids. If you and the parent had very specific roles you played in your kids' lives you may find that it is a challenge to have the other parent's role now empty. First of all, you are enough. You don't have to be two parents. Secondly, this also gives you the chance to do things you never did before. Maybe the other parent always took your daughter to softball practice or your son to drama club. Now you may have the opportunity to do those things and may find that that you enjoy it and it richens your relationship with your kid.

You Do Not Have to Do This Alone

If you need help, ask for it. You don't have to be a superhero. Call on your family and close friends to help you. You may find you are facing jobs or tasks around the house that the other parent always did that you are not skilled at. Ask for help and if there are things around the house you don't know how to do, learn so you can become self-sufficient. Also remember that your kids can step up and help with things around the house.

Ask for family and friends to babysit or do things with your child. Do not be afraid to ask the other parent to help. If you need a babysitter, see if he or she is available. Ask the other parent to handle some things—taking your child to the doctor, for a haircut, shopping for new shoes, to a school activity, or on outings with the child's friends. Doing so will give you a break, help the other parent feel involved and important, and let your child know he or she still has two parents who take responsibility for him or her.

Plan for all eventualities. For example, you're at work and your kid is sick and needs to come home. You can't leave. It's your week to parent. Who are you going to call to get your kid?

Look through the list of resources in Appendix B at the end of this book to find organizations, websites, and books that can provide you with additional support.

STRATEGIES FOR MANAGING AS A SINGLE PARENT

- Take things one day at a time.
- Do not expect to be perfect.
- Ask for help from family, friends, and the other parent.
- Continue to have friends and activities that make you happy.
- Do not be afraid of being alone and take some time to get used to it.
- Make to do lists to help you get organized around the house.
- Use a calendar to stay organized.
- Remember that your child is adjusting to things just as you are.
- Do not take on too much or overschedule yourself out of the fear of being lonely.
- Make time for your child.
- Include your child in some decisions around the house.
- Keep your child involved in daily family life.
- Do not make drastic changes too soon. Take time to decide what will be best for you and your child.
- Remember that you are not doing anything new, you're just doing it in a different way. You will be able to cope.
- Enjoy the new freedom you may have and don't feel guilty.

Chapter 11

Dealing with Other People

Divorce or separation is a very personal matter. While going through the process, you probably realized that more people were involved in your personal matter than you ever dreamed possible. Now that you are through the process and are living with your parenting plan, you will find that you are not done with other people's involvement in your relationship with your child.

Schools

It's essential that your child's school know about the divorce or separation. Divorce and separation can affect children's performance and behavior in school, and it is important your child's teacher have this information. You will also want to be sure that the school has up-to-date addresses and phone numbers for you and the other parent. If the other parent has the right to access your child's school records (and almost all nonresidential parents have this right), the school will need to be notified. You can let the other parent do this or you can do it yourself if you would like.

You can contact your child's school and ask that separate parent/teacher conferences be scheduled for you and the other parent. If you are comfortable

Parenting Together Apart: For the Residential Parent

attending one conference together, you may still do so. Discuss with the other parent whether he or she will attend school events and whether you will sit together.

Keep in mind that contact with your child's teacher is not an opportunity to complain about the other parent, blame things on the other parent, or pump the teacher for information about the other parent. The teacher can offer insight as to how your child is adjusting to the change in home life and how it is impacting his or her school performance. If your child consistently has problems the day after a transition between parents, this is an indication that there are some adjustment issues you need to deal with. Take a look at the timing of the transitions. Would it be easier for the child if he or she came home a bit earlier? Would the adjustment be better if the other parent took the child to school instead of returning him or her home the night before? Take a look at what changes you can make and try different things so that you can find what works best.

To help make things simpler in your dealings with the school, it may be a good idea to agree on some rules about which parent will be responsible for what. For example, it makes sense that the parent who has the child for the day in question is the one to sign a permission slip for a field trip or after school event. If your child is going to be with the other parent from Wednesday night to Saturday morning and the school sends home a permission slip for a field trip that will happen on Friday, it may make sense to let the other parent be the one to sign it. Of course, both parents need to know about it, in case of emergency or in case there is a change in the parenting schedule.

Additionally, children sometimes are required to get a signature from a parent on a test or report card. You can decide that one of you will always be solely responsible for this, or you can decide that whichever parent is with the child when he or she comes home from school with the item will be the one to sign it. Make sure the parent who is not signing has a chance to see the report card or test. Some parents decide that one parent will handle all paperwork for the sport the child plays and the other parent will handle all school paperwork. If you can have a standard plan in place for these things, you can prevent confusion.

As the residential parent, you probably have the most contact with the school and are the one who gets most of the school related correspondence and graded homework papers. You might consider saving some of these papers for your child to share with the other parent. It will help him or her feel in the loop and give your child positive reinforcement for work well done.

Even though you are the one who has the most contact with the school, it is not your responsibility to be the other parent's liaison with the school. He or she must develop a relationship with the school and teacher on his or her own. While it is nice to send things along you think he or she might be interested in, it is not your responsibility to remind him or her to sign up for a parent-teacher conference or to look up the school calendar. Provide information you know your child would like to share and then get out of the way and let the other parent step up—or not. It's out of your control and you are not his or her keeper.

If you have sole legal custody of your child the other parent can still have contact with the school and be informed about happenings and events and see report cards, but he or she doesn't have the right to make decisions for your child. So in this situation, you are the only one who would sign permission slips or agree to a special education plan for your child. You are also the only one who would be allowed to take the child home from school for illness.

Health Care Workers

You should contact your child's doctor(s) and dentist to inform them about the divorce or separation. This is particularly important information for a pediatrician to have, because the emotions your child experiences during the post-divorce period can have an impact on his or her health. Be sure the office has up-to-date addresses and phone numbers for both parents. You'll also want to be sure to let them know about any changes in insurance and responsibility for the medical or dental bills. Make sure that you and the other parent both have health insurance cards for your child, so either of you can get medical care for him or her at any time.

The other parent may request that the doctor separately inform him or her about your child's health, if he or she was given the right to access your child's medical information. Some parents take turns accompanying children on medical and dental appointments so that both have a chance to speak to the health care professionals. Think about this option and discuss it with the other parent.

If you have sole legal custody, this can mean that a doctor or hospital may not allow the other parent to authorize medical care for your child (but many practices will treat your child no matter who brings him in if he needs immediate care). This can be a real problem if you cannot be reached or are out of town while your child is with the other parent. If you feel that you want the other parent to be able to authorize medical care, then it is a good idea to give him or her written authorization (and have it notarized). Give a copy of this signed and notarized form to the other parent, to your child's pediatrician and dentist (and other doctors your child sees regularly), and to the school. If you do NOT want the other parent to have the ability to make any medical decisions make sure you let all the health care providers know this.

AUTHORIZATION TO OBTAIN MEDICAL CARE

I, _____ am the mother/father of the child _____, whose date of birth is _____. I have sole custody of the child. I hereby authorize _____, the mother/father of the child, to make medical/dental/health decisions about the child and to authorize treatment for the child in my absence or if I cannot be reached.

_____
print your name

_____ _____
sign your name   date

Your Family and Friends

Now that you are divorced or separated, your family and friends are more important than ever to you. Your family and close friends are also an important part of your child's support system. While you want your child to continue to have contact with these people, you need to strike a balance. If you fill the time you spend with your child by always having a friend or relative over to your home, you are sending a message that you do not want to be alone with your child. Involve your child with your family and friendships, but make sure you have time alone to maintain your own relationship. It is fine to have a friend drop over for a few hours or go to dinner with your family. However, you are using your friends and family as a crutch if you need them with you all the time.

It's important to strike a balance. And keep in mind that your relationships with family and friends will likely change now that you are single. You might gravitate towards single friends. You might avoid a certain aunt who was not supportive during your divorce. Do what feels right.

The Other Parent's Family and Friends

Just as it is important for your child to have contact with your family and friends, he or she needs to remain in contact with the other parent's family and friends. Refrain from making negative or derogatory comments about any of these people no matter how you feel about them. Listen to your child talk about the visits with these people and participate in the conversation, but do not press your child for details or be overly inquisitive. In short, it's none of your business.

Some parents waste a lot of time and energy worrying and being upset about what happens at the other grandparent's home. If your child is not in danger while there, there isn't much you can do about these visits. You might not like the fact that their grandmother always gives them candy or that their grandfather is always watching NASCAR while they are there, but you have no right to dictate to these people as long as your child is safe, as hard as that might be to accept.

Parenting Together Apart: For the Residential Parent

If you find that the other parent is always with family or friends when your child is there, this is something you might want to calmly discuss alone with him or her. Point out that you don't mind that he or she brings the child along sometimes, but that you want him or her to know that the child also needs alone time. Be aware that some nonresidential parents use other people as a crutch when they don't feel confident enough to be alone with their child. You may need to help the other parent develop some confidence.

Should you run into any of these former relatives or former friends, be polite but distant (and remember that you're going to see your ex's extended family at graduations and weddings so you want to maintain a friendly relationship). Do not get into a discussion about the divorce, separation, or about the parenting schedule. The details of these things are for you and the other parent only. You do not need to justify or explain anything to your former relatives or former friends. Doing so will likely only result in bad feelings or conflict.

Your New Partner

If you have someone new in your life that is important to you, do some evaluating before involving that person with your child. If you are at a point where you are casually dating different people, it's best not to introduce them all to your child—at least not in a serious way. It is okay for you to date and for your child to know that you do. You are supposed to go on living! But you don't want your child to form an attachment to someone who won't be around. And you definitely don't want your child to get close to lots of different people, only to have them leave your life.

If you have one person you are seeing regularly, decide how serious you are about the new relationship. If you think this person is important to you, it is fine to introduce him or her to your child and allow him or her to get to know your child. You should never present the new person as a replacement for the other parent and it is very important that you continue to have time alone with your child. Children and teens will be curious about this new relationship and may ask if you plan on remarrying. It's best to be honest, but don't go into the details about your relationship. You should also expect your child to exhibit some resentment, coldness, or rudeness towards this person. This will pass with time (which doesn't make it any easier but at least you can know it is normal and will pass).

Make your own personal and moral judgment about a new partner spending the night with you when your child is present unless your custody order specifically states you are not allowed to have partners sleepover when your child is there. It is never appropriate for a child to witness overt adult sexual behavior.

DATING TIPS
- Date if you feel it is something you are ready for and comfortable with.
- Do not get your child deeply involved with all of the different people you date if you are playing the field.
- Be honest with your child about the fact that you are dating.
- Expect your child to have mixed emotions about you dating.
- Introduce your child to someone that is special with whom you are having (or hoping to have) a long-term relationship.
- Decide if you feel sleepovers with dates are appropriate when your child is at your home.
- Never make your child feel as if your new partner is somehow a replacement for the other parent, and do not place him or her in a parental role or allow him or her to discipline your child.
- Do not let your dating life fill all of your free time with your child.
- Do insist on respectful, polite behavior but don't be surprised if your child is resentful.
- Do not expect your child to be thrilled you are dating or to accept a new partner quickly.
- Do not let your child feel he is competing with your new partner for your attention.

- Never allow your child to witness adult sexual activity.
- Do not make your new partner a part of the family too quickly.
- Do not discuss your dating life with the other parent or expect him or her to discuss his or hers with you.
- Do not get your child involved in your emotional roller coaster. He or she is not a confidant or pal. Keep any romantic angst to yourself
- Remember that while you are supposed to have an adult social life, you want your child to feel cared for and important.

Stepfamilies

Should you reach the point where you are going to remarry, you need to set some ground rules. The new spouse should never be referred to as mom or dad, or whatever name the child uses for the other parent. The new spouse can have authority over the child since they will be sharing the same house, but you as the parent should be the one making all the important decisions about the child.

If there are stepsiblings, you need for your child to know he or she is not being replaced and is still your child who is of prime importance in your life. The same goes for any half siblings that are later born into the family. Don't expect the stepsiblings to become BFFs. Even if they immediately have fun together, there will be deep-seated emotions to contend with. Building a stepfamily is complex and takes time.

See the resources in Appendix B for information and support as you form a stepfamily.

The Other Parent's New Partner

If the other parent is dating, you should not be involved. It may be difficult, and you may feel hurt and betrayed, but you have to stay out of it. If your child talks about the new partner, it is fine to listen, but don't make snide comments, ask questions, or get involved in any way. If the other parent begins dating one person seriously, you will certainly hear more about it. Don't believe everything your child says. If you run into the person, be civil and polite.

If your child is witnessing inappropriate adult sexual activity at the other parent's home, your first step should be (as always) to talk to the other parent. You can't believe everything your child is telling you. Express your concerns to the other parent. If you still believe that this is occurring, or your child continues to tell you about other instances, then you need to talk to your attorney if your discussions with the other parent have not improved the situation. Another option is to contact your local department of social or human services or state child abuse hotline.

If your child has complaints about the new partner, it's something that has to be worked out in that household. While it might be ok for you to give the other parent a head's up, it isn't your job to mediate the problem or solve it.

Should the other parent remarry, you can expect your child to be excited, happy, depressed, nervous, left out, angry, jealous, and so on. Your child will need reassurance that he or she will always be an important person to both you and the other parent. Remember that no stepparent can ever take your place or fill your shoes. It is not acceptable for the new stepparent to be called by the same name as your child calls you ("Mom," "Daddy," "Ma," "Father," etc.), and if this is happening, you should have a polite and calm conversation with your child's other parent to express how you feel. If your child is the one who began calling the new partner by this name, tell him or her how important your relationship is and explain that it hurts your feelings that this is happening. Ultimately, the other parent will be the one who will have to resolve this issue, since it is happening in his or her home. Adjusting to a new stepparent will take time and you need to be patient with your child while this is happening.

As hard as it may be, try to view the new partner as an ally. He or she will be spending time with your child and will likely interact with your child and do some things for your kid that a parent would do (make meals, put a bandage on, play games). If you view the new partner as an enemy it helps none of you. If instead you can find a way to be friendly and accepting, you may be able to work together for the benefit of your child. It's normal to feel jealous and suspicious of this person who is spending a lot of time with your kid. Ultimately you have to trust your ex to pick a reasonable person. Try to be glad that there is another person who cares for your child and who is there for him. The more the better when it comes to that.

TIPS FOR STEPFAMILY PARENTING

- Do not expect your child to be thrilled about your remarriage.
- Explain to your child that the new spouse is not a replacement for the other parent.
- Help your child get to know stepsiblings before a marriage.
- Expect conflict in your stepfamily and take the time to work through it.
- Do not ask or allow your child to call the new stepparent by the same name he or she calls the other parent.
- Make sure your child knows that he or she is an important part of the new family.
- Help the new spouse develop a relationship with your child. Do not expect them to have a parent-child relationship. The relationship cannot immediately take on this form. Eventually, your child may come to see the stepparent as a third parent.
- Allow the stepparent to have reasonable authority over your child, but make sure everyone in the family remembers that you are the child's parent.
- Take the time to listen to your child's feelings and thoughts about the new marriage.
- Continue to respect your child's visitation schedule and make sure that it is a priority in your family.
- If the new spouse has children, try to rearrange scheduling so that all of the children can be together sometimes. They will never develop good relationships if they hardly ever see each other.

- Take the time to make your new marriage as successful as possible. Another divorce isn't going to be good for anyone.
- Get support from a stepfamily association or a counselor experienced in stepfamily issues if necessary.
- Make sure your child is an involved, active, and important member of your new family.

Chapter 12

Special Situations

Each family is unique and no one experiences the exact same set of problems. This chapter will help you work through some specific problems that may be unique to your family.

Physical or Sexual Abuse

If your child has actually been, or you honestly believe he or she may have been, physically or sexually abused by the other parent (or by anyone else for that matter), you must first obtain whatever emergency medical care is needed. Usually, this means getting the child to a hospital or doctor immediately. You need to contact your state's social services department or the police to report the abuse. (State abuse hotline numbers are listed in Appendix D.) You then will need to cooperate with the caseworkers who investigate the report. Obtain counseling for your child to assist with the mental and emotional damage that has been done. Contact your attorney to find out if you should seek sole custody or have visitation supervised. When your child is in immediate danger, all visitation plans must be cancelled until you can get to the bottom of things.

Substance Abuse

If the other parent has developed a substance abuse problem, you need to consult your attorney about how to deal with the situation. You may be able to request drug testing and treatment before visitation time is allowed to resume.

If you have developed a substance abuse problem, it is important that you get help. Talk to your child about your problem, what you are doing about it, and how you got into this situation. Encourage him or her to avoid making the same mistakes.

If you suspect or know that your child is using drugs, it is imperative that you get him or her help immediately. (There are some organizations and information clearinghouses listed in Appendix B that can help you with this.) You need to speak with the other parent immediately so you can work together to solve this, if possible. Get a referral to a treatment center or substance abuse counselor from your child's pediatrician. You can contact law enforcement, but this should only be a last resort.

Mental Illness

It is normal for your child to react to the divorce or separation and resulting adjustment with anger, depression, fear, regression (acting younger than the child is), sadness, guilt, and so on. For some children, these reactions might be quite severe. There is a fine line between a normal reaction to the divorce and an abnormal reaction. If your child endangers him- or herself or threatens to harm him- or herself, you need to get mental health assistance immediately. If your child's attitude and emotions seem to make it impossible for him or her to live a normal life, you need to get help. (Chapter 2 lists the symptoms of depression. Consult that list if depression is a concern.)

SIGNS YOU MAY NEED TO GET HELP FOR YOUR CHILD
- He or she is extremely detached and displays very little emotion or reaction to anything.

Parenting Together Apart: For the Residential Parent

- He or she talks about suicide or harming him- or herself, or actually attempts self-harm.
- He or she is frequently violent and destructive.
- He or she is withdrawn, sad, or depressed.
- He or she is overly nervous, obsessive, or compulsive.
- He or she cries far more than is normal for the age.
- He or she is constantly hostile to you or the other parent.
- He or she is experiencing serious difficulty at school (and this is a new problem).
- He or she has regressed substantially and has remained so for a long time.

Note: These are some general warning signs. Only a trained mental health worker can know if your child needs treatment. These descriptions are basic and are not determinative. It is normal for a child to display some of these signs (but self-harm is never normal) in a mild way when coping with divorce, separation, and visitation. You should be concerned if you see these symptoms on a long-term consistent basis. If you are ever in doubt, seek assistance from a mental health worker or consult your child's pediatrician.

You know your child. If you feel that his or her reaction is just not right, get help. It is a good idea to talk to the other parent about this. Working together is the best way to handle the situation. If there is any question in your mind as to whether your child would benefit from mental health assistance, then you should err on the side of caution and get help. Your child's pediatrician can make a referral to a counselor or therapist. A child who does not need therapy will be identified by the therapist, so you won't do any harm by taking your child to a therapist.

If you feel that you are experiencing depression, anxiety, or other mental health problems, seek help. There are many treatments available and it is important to recognize that these are real illnesses, just like pneumonia or asthma, and there are treatments available. Don't worry about what other people think. You cannot be an adequate parent if your own problems go untreated.

If the other parent exhibits signs of mental illness, you need to contact your attorney. Family and friends may be able to support your suspicions about this. Do not involve your child! If you feel your child is unsafe at the other parent's home, contact the child abuse hotline for your area and speak to your attorney about temporarily stopping visitation.

Violation of the Terms of the Custody Order

If the other parent is continuously and grossly late for the pick-up or drop-off, and you have tried discussing this with him or her to no avail, you need to talk to your attorney. Keep in mind that the goal should be to set up a schedule that can be followed by both of you. Your goal is not to punish the other parent or attempt to keep him or her away from your child. You do not want to keep him or her away from your child, but instead want to create a schedule that can be followed reliably. Visitation is something that is good for your child, so you should try to work with the other parent to find a schedule that can be followed. (Chapter 7 has more information about this.)

If the other parent fails to bring your child back from visitation and you are fairly certain this is not just a slight delay, you should first call the other parent and ask if there has been a schedule mix up. If he or she refuses to return your child, or if you cannot locate him or her and you feel that this could be an abduction situation, you need to contact the police and your attorney immediately.

Bad Parenting by the Other Parent

Almost all divorced or separated parents, at some time or another, have reservations about the other parent's parenting abilities. If you're honest with yourself, you've probably had doubts about your own parenting abilities at some point in your life as well. No one is perfect, after all. Just because you do not agree with the decisions or actions of the other parent does not mean that he or she is an unfit parent. It is helpful to remember that at some point, you did believe he or she was a good parent, otherwise you would not have chosen to have a child with him or her.

That being said, there are people who are simply terrible parents. If the other parent is part of this group, you need to ask yourself why you did not act on it during the divorce. If nothing has changed between then and now, perhaps you are just feeling very angry, hurt, or depressed. If you believed this was true, why didn't you take steps to protect your child then? How serious are the problems?

Sometimes people change after a divorce. Some people even develop mental illnesses after a divorce. If this has happened with the other parent, you should contact your attorney to discuss your options, which may include seeking reduced or supervised visitation. It is also very important that you document everything you can-keep a log or diary of the incidents that have concerned you and obtain copies of all medical or school records that will support your case. Do not involve your child at this stage. If you do return to court or mediation, you will need to tell your child this is happening and provide a brief explanation, such as, "Mom/Dad and I are having some differences of opinion about where you should spend your time, and we are asking the judge to help us."

If you thought that the other parent was a terrible parent before the divorce or separation, and you did all you could to let the court know, but feel that you weren't taken seriously or that the visitation that was ordered is simply too much considering the other parent's abilities, you must talk to your attorney. You should keep track of all problems and concerns (in a log or journal) so that you can return to court in the future with more proof and convince the judge to see things your way.

While necessary in some situations, this kind of approach will ensure that your relationship with the other parent continues to be difficult and will impact your child.

Nonpayment of Child Support

If the other parent is supposed to pay you child support and is consistently late or misses payments, you need to speak to your attorney or to your state child support collection unit. It is very important that both you and the other parent understand that child support is not tied to visitation. If the other parent doesn't pay child support, this does not mean you can deny him or her visitation. The two things are completely separate.

Sometimes nonresidential parents think that they can reduce child support if they spend more time with the child. For example, if you go out of town for a week and you and the other parent agree that he or she will care for the child in your absence, child support still must be paid for that week, even though the other parent is the one who is caring for the child. In some states, child support is directly related to the amount of scheduled time the parents have so if you make a permanent change to the schedule, you may need to adjust the child support to match it. Check with your attorney about your state laws.

The other parent cannot dictate how you spend child support money. Spending it on the mortgage or on car repairs is perfectly fine—you could even go spend it on a new pair of shoes for yourself if you really want. You do have an obligation to make sure your child is supported and to make sure he or she is cared for adequately, so it only makes sense to try to use child support money to do so.

In general, try to keep child support issues separate from visitation issues and make sure you do not get your child involved in child support problems. Try not to let child support disputes poison your parenting relationship.

Changing Custody

After living as a residential parent for a while, some parents come to the conclusion that the arrangement is not working. If this happens to you, think about why you feel this way. Is your child consistently unhappy? If so, try some therapy or take a look at scheduling issues that might be disruptive or upsetting. Are you unhappy? Many divorced parents do experience feelings of unhappiness, but it does go away-by itself or with therapy. Look at what is upsetting you about the situation and try to change things. Moving your child over to live with the other parent may not be the best solution for any of you. Not only will it shake things up yet again, but it is not something that is easy to undo once you make the change. If you are feeling like you need more time to yourself see if the other parent is able to extend visitation times temporarily to see if this helps. Get help from friends and family. Make some lifestyle changes so you are not so stressed out. If none of this is possible, or it doesn't solve the underlying problem, contact your attorney.

Sometimes a change in custody can be a solution and if this is what will work best for your child and your family, you should not feel guilty or upset about it. Getting your attorney involved will often mean a return to court, and this will have an effect on your child. Children are aware of court proceedings simply because it is almost impossible to hide it from them. Also, your child may be assigned a law guardian or guardian ad litem who will represent him or her in court. This attorney will need to meet with and speak to your child. It is always best to try to work something out on your own without a return to court. If you and the other parent just cannot find a compromise, try using a mediator. Your child does not need to be involved in mediation as he or she is in a formal court proceeding.

You Want to End Visitation

Some residential parents feel overwhelmed and frustrated with the demands of a parenting plan. They are tired of dealing with the other parent, tired of trading the child back and forth, and just want visitation to disappear. They decide that they never want to see the other parent, they never want to speak to him or her again, and they want no more visitation. They may decide that the other parent is a bad influence or doesn't add anything to the child's life.

Remember that your child needs to have a second parent in his or her life whether you like him or her or not. Make some changes to make things easier on yourself. Ask that the other parent not come in the house when picking up or dropping off the child. Simply refuse to argue with him or her. Agree to speak with him or her only when someone else you trust is present. If you must, have all schedule changes or negotiations handled by your attorney. Do whatever you have to do to ensure that your child will have two parents while reducing the stress you are under.

If reducing conflict with the other parent doesn't work, consider all the possibilities of what else is really bothering you. Are you not getting enough sleep? Is your schedule too crowded? Are you worried about money? Are you having too many conflicts with the other parent? Are you and your child having conflicts? Try to get at the root of the problem and see if you can fix it. If you don't see what you can change, try seeing a therapist. He or she may be able to help you change things to make them easier to cope with.

You have to realize that the other parent is not going to change, and since visitation is a basic fact of life now, you have to find some way to deal with it. Whatever you do, don't give up. When you created this child, you gave an unbreakable lifetime commitment to always do your best to love and care for him or her, and this includes making sure your child has a second parent. Living with a parenting plan isn't easy and all parents struggle with it at some point. Try to focus on the positives and do what you can to make things bearable. Remember that you're doing all of this for your child.

Supervised Visitation

Some nonresidential parents are only permitted to have supervised visitation with their children. This means that another adult, who is approved by the court, must be present during parenting time. Sometimes supervised visitation happens at an actual supervised visitation program, but more often it just happens in the presence of another adult (usually a relative) that both parents trust. If the other parent has supervised visitation, you probably had a good reason for requesting it or the judge had a good reason for ordering it.

In most cases, supervised visitation does not go on forever, and if the other parent proves that he or she can handle visitation (and has resolved the issues that led to it such as substance abuse), the visits become unsupervised. The goal really is to help the other parent reach a point where he or she can have normal access to the child. Many nonresidential parents are required to attend parenting classes, support groups, or therapy to help prepare them for this.

A child who goes to supervised visitation may be confused and may not understand why he or she cannot see the other parent anywhere else. Explain to your child that this is where he or she will be seeing Mom/Dad at least for a while because that is how the judge decided visitation is to happen. Don't make yourself out as the bad guy by explaining that it was what you wanted, too. You need to encourage your child to go to visitation and have a good time with the other parent. You should not quiz him or her about how the visits went. Contact the person who is supervising visitation if you want a report. If you have a problem with the person who is supervising the visitation or the location where it is taking place, try to come up with some alternatives and contact your attorney about them.

If the other parent has a history of violence or instability, it can be difficult to take your child to supervised visitation even though the judge has decided that it is what is best. It is important that you reassure yourself that your child will be safe. If visitation is at a facility, familiarize yourself with it first. Talk to the person who will be supervising and get a sense for how carefully things are monitored and what kinds of activities will happen. Once you have done this, you simply have to let go and allow your child to go. Stay in touch with the supervisor and your attorney, so you can monitor the situation.

Gender and Sexuality

If you or your ex explores or makes decisions about sexuality or gender after or during the divorce or separation, explain things in age-appropriate terms your child can understand. If you don't approve of the choices the other parent is making, try to remember that it is not your place to judge. Changes or adjustments in sexuality or gender have no bearing on a person's parenting ability, or on the close bond that exists with your child. If you find your child is struggling with the changes, take him or her to a therapist. It is completely normal for a child to have difficulty adjusting to a parent who is transitioning or who has come out. If your ex is in this situation, your role is to be supportive of the other parent and of your child. Listen to your child if he or she has questions or concerns. Do not criticize the other parent in front of your child. It's completely normal for you to have mixed feelings about the situation, but try to work through those yourself and present a supportive face to your child.

Teens

If you are the parent of a teen, you know that everything is different for teens. You probably had to modify your house rules, your discipline style, and even your communication style when your child became a teen. Teens handle divorce differently from children of any other age. While they do experience the same feelings of loss, grief, anger, sadness, etc., they deal with it in different ways and put blame on themselves for the divorce. Many also see the divorce as proof that they will never have a stable relationship and that they should never get married. You will need to work through these feelings with your teen and help him or her realize that no one is to blame for the divorce and that it is not a predictor of the child's future relationships.

Teens need to be consulted about parenting plans and schedules. They are at a point in their lives where their friends are the most important thing in the world and they are also working very hard to be independent of their parents. While teens should have input, they should not be permitted to make the final decisions.

As you begin to implement your parenting plan involving your teen, you will meet with resistance, outbursts, and even refusals to communicate. Your parenting plan is flexible, but it is not optional. Allowances can be made for your teen's schedule, job, and friends, but the bottom line is that the plan must be basically honored. (More information about teens is contained in Chapter 13.) With that being said, there is very little you can do to force a teen to comply with the schedule.

Parents Who Refuse to Exercise Visitation

Sometimes parents arrive late or forget about visitation. This is normal. Talk with the other parent about your concerns. Other times, parents simply do not show up for visitation time and time again. If this happens, try directly asking the other parent why this is happening. You should keep a record of these occurrences. You do not have to cover for the other parent or try to make excuses for his or her absence. It is okay to tell your child you don't know why he or she did not come, but it is not okay for you to fly off the handle in front of your child.

If your child's other parent consistently and regularly is skipping visitation without calling or rescheduling, you need to consult your attorney. You are also going to need to get your child some help from a therapist or counselor. Being abandoned by a parent is traumatic, and you need to make sure your child has the support necessary to cope with this situation.

It is okay to be honest with your child about what is happening. Explain that the other parent, for some reason, is missing visitation. Help your child understand that it is not the child's fault and that the parent must have some problems he or she needs to work through. Explain that it is okay to feel hurt or angry. Continue to try to encourage the other parent to exercise the same visitation. If this is a long standing problem it may make sense to get the schedule changed so that you and your kid are not left waiting at the front door every week for someone who doesn't show up.

Things that Supercede Visitation

There are situations that will essentially supercede your schedule:

- a seriously ill or hospitalized child;
- extreme weather conditions that prevent travel;
- family emergencies;
- a parent's serious illness; or,
- death of a close family member.

If there is a weather emergency that makes it unsafe to travel, the child should stay where he or she is. You can resume your normal schedule after it is over. The child should have phone contact (if possible) with the other parent. If either you or the other parent is ill and unable to care for your child, the healthy parent can step in, and help can also be found from relatives and friends. Children should have regular ongoing contact with seriously ill parents. Should a family member pass away, your child, if he or she is old enough, will want to be able to be with that side of the family and attend gatherings and services. Make adjustments to the schedule to allow for this.

Other unexpected situations can arise, such as a parent being delayed by a car accident or an emergency at work. You and the other parent should try to be flexible in these situations. The important thing is to make sure your child is not frightened by the unexpected change or delay. Try to reschedule to compensate for the unexpected change.

A Sick Child

If your child is quite ill, you should try to arrange for the other parent to see him or her, but this shouldn't be done according to the schedule. Instead fit in visits depending on your child's condition. Short, frequent visits work best. If the child is in the hospital, you can take turns staying there at different parts of the day. Seriously ill children need support from and contact with both parents on a regular basis. If your child is home sick from school this doesn't necessarily mean visitation is off. If your child can travel, the other parent is absolutely able to care for a cold and should be given the chance to. If your child is very insistent about staying home, talk with the other parent. Maybe he or she can stop over for a visit.

If the child has a high fever or has a gastrointestinal illness, it is probably best if you reschedule because no one wants to be shuffled from house to house in that condition. If your child is highly contagious with something like strep throat or chickenpox it may be wise for him or her to stay put until the period ends (check with your pediatrician). If you must leave town or for some reason and cannot care for the child, talk to the other parent about him or her coming to stay with the child at your home. If this will not work, the other parent will need to take the child with him or her and make the child as comfortable as possible.

A child with a minor illness, such as a cold, is able to go as planned and be cared for by the other parent. Pack medication and anything else that will keep your child comfortable. Do what you can to make sure your child will be cared for properly and then let it go. Most nonresidential parents are capable of caring for a sick child. A sniffle is not a good reason to cancel visitation. You are both parents and are both able to care for common childhood ailments.

Relocation

Relocation is one of the top questions I am asked about when it comes to child custody. It's a huge issue and one you are not alone in dealing with. There may come a point in your life where you find you need or want to move to another area. The first thing you need to do is consult your attorney. There are limits on your ability to move. Often, a custody agreement or judgment will contain specific restrictions about the residential parent's ability to relocate. The law in many states limits your right to relocation if you are the residential parent and requires court permission or agreement by the nonresidential parent.

If you are not able to get clearance to move, you will need to carefully weigh your choices. You can stay where you are and find some way to make it work, or you might find that you have no choice but to leave. If you are not permitted to take your child with you, then you may find yourself trading places with the other parent—with you becoming the nonresidential parent. If this is the case, you need to flip this book over and read the other side. Remember that there is nothing wrong with being the nonresidential parent and that you can continue to have an excellent relationship with your child no matter how far apart you live.

Special Needs Children

If you have a special needs child, you are probably a bit apprehensive about visitation. Make sure that the other parent is educated about the child's needs, medications, emergency care, diet, and so on. It is a good idea to write all of this information down and make sure it travels with the child. You might also suggest that the other parent talk with the child's doctor or therapist to fully understand the child's limitations and necessary care. Make sure that the child's medications travel with him or her. Get both parents involved in the plan the school creates for your child, so you both are in the loop.

Special needs are not an excuse to limit visitation. These children need both parents just as much as other children do.

Food Allergies

If your child has a food allergy, you are on high alert for all possible dangers. If your ex is on board with everything, co-parenting shouldn't change that. If you learn new things (based on new research or something your child's doctor tells you), share it with the other parent. Be clear about which parent is responsible for notifying the school, coaches, and friends' parents.

If the other parent does not believe your child has an allergy, doesn't accept it, or refuses to fully understand your first step is to try to educate him. Suggest he talk to the pediatrician about it or offer some online resources for reading. If you make no progress and the other parent refuses to ensure your child is safe, you need to talk to your attorney as this could be a reason for a change in custody. As you know, food allergies are no joke and any parent who refuses to take them seriously is going to have a difficult time in front of a judge. Document everything you can to prove your case.

Parental Abduction

Parental abduction accounts for the majority of missing children. Should this ever happen in your family, immediately contact the police with a recent photo of your child (and of the other parent if you believe he or she is involved). Obtain a copy of your judgment or order that gives you custody and provide this to the police.

One way to prevent abduction out of the country is to apply for a passport for your child and keep it in a safety deposit box. Only one passport per person can be issued. You can also sign up for the Child Passport Issuance Alert system (see appendix) which will alert you if a passport application is submitted for your child.

Local police often sponsor child safety days, where they will photograph and fingerprint children. If you are truly concerned that abduction is a real possibility, then you must notify your child's school, caregivers, and relatives that they do not have permission to release your child to the other parent. If you are concerned about abduction, it is important that you talk to your attorney and explain your fears and what has caused you to feel this way and discuss your legal option. If abduction is seen as a real possibility, the court can require parents to post bonds with the court which are surrendered if they do abduct and can be used to pay the expenses involved in getting the child back. (Appendices B and C contain lists of organizations that can assist you should this ever happen.)

Military Personnel/Travel for Work

If the other parent is in the military or travels for work, he or she may be away for long periods of time. When the other parent is in the area, your child will want to spend time with him or her. It's important that you remain flexible and encourage visitation when it is possible.

If you are a member of the military or travel for your job, you need to make child care arrangements for when you are away. The military provides a family care plan you can complete. Consider using the other parent as the caregiver. If you use another caregiver, make sure he or she is clear about the visitation schedule. Be aware that it is very possible the other parent could ask to have the parenting plan changed so he or she has residential custody while you are away. To stay close to your child when you are away, review the tips in the chapter on long-distance parenting in the nonresidential parent half of this book.

Imprisonment

Should the other parent be imprisoned, this is sure to be a very difficult situation for your child who may be confused, hurt, or angry. You will probably be angry, resentful, and disgusted by this situation, and your first instinct will be to completely shield your child from the other parent. However, you cannot hide the fact that the other parent is in prison. If you don't explain where he or she is, your child will think the other parent has just disappeared and lost interest in him or her. Explain to your child in an age-appropriate way where the other parent is and why. It is okay to say that he or she did something wrong or broke a law, since this is the fact of the matter. Answer your child's questions.

Whether your child will visit the other parent will depend in part on where the prison is located. If it is located nearby, an in-person visit can be arranged. The thought of taking your child to a prison may horrify you, but it is important that he or she continue to have contact with the other parent. Your child needs to see that the other parent exists, still loves him or her, and is sorry for making the bad decision that led to the prison sentence. This really can be a good experience for your child and can emphasize the importance of making good decisions.

Many prisons have special children's visitation programs. Call the prison and ask about this or check some of the resources in Appendices B and C. Some of these programs arrange for visitation in a somewhat nonthreatening and child-friendly area. If you do take your child for a prison visit, you do need to prepare him or her what for will happen and what will be seen. Try to explain how a prison works and that there are guards and other inmates. Even teens need some preparation before visiting a prison. They may have to go through a metal detector and remove their shoes before being allowed entry. If you show fear or apprehension about the visit, your child will as well. If you can remain calm and matter of fact about it, your child is likely to handle it well.

If you are completely opposed to taking your child to the prison, be aware that the other parent may decide to request a court order forcing you to bring the child for visitation. You need to speak to your attorney should this happen. If you live too far away or if you decide not to bring the child to the prison, he or she may maintain contact with the other parent by mail.

Stay at Home Parents

If you are a stay at home parent, suddenly having your child gone for periods of time can be upsetting and distracting. You may want to try to schedule other things for the days your child is with the other parent so you don't feel you are at a complete loss.

Homeschooling

If you are homeschooling your child you will need to set up the schooling schedule around your ex's parenting time. It is possible that you can homeschool together, each taking responsibility for different subjects. Generally though one parent handles homeschooling. You are absolutely within your rights to send homework with your child when he goes to the other parent's home.

If Your Child Is Adopted

If your child was adopted (either by both of you, or was the natural child of one and adopted by the other parent), you should follow the advice offered in this book. Simply because one or both of you is not the child's biological parent should not alter or change anything.

When the child was adopted, he or she legally became your child, with both of you as his or her parents. A divorce, separation, or end of relationship cannot change that. An adoption cannot be undone.

If your child knows that he or she was adopted (as most children do these days), he or she may wonder if the divorce or separation means that somehow the adoption will come undone as well. Make sure that you reassure him or her that this cannot happen and that both of you will continue to be parents in his or her life forever. For some teens, a divorce or separation can spur him or her to try to locate his or her biological parents. Should this issue come up, you should discuss it with your child and offer him or her support, whatever he or she decides to do. It is important to remember that if the biological parents are located, they cannot take your place in your child's life.

Grandparent Visitation

Grandparent visitation has received some publicity in recent years. Many times when there is a divorce or separation, the parents of the nonresidential parent make noise about requesting grandparent visitation. The fact is that it is very difficult to get a court to order grandparent visitation. However, just because it is unlikely a court will order you to provide grandparent visitation, does not mean you shouldn't agree to it.

Grandparents are an important part of a child's life, and to deny time to the grandparents is really to deprive your child of this important relationship. It's likely that you and your former in-laws harbor unpleasant feelings towards each other. Remember though that when you deal with them that you should focus on what your child needs and not about your disagreements with your former relatives. You probably feel like you don't have enough time with your child, and to give up one weekend a month to people you dislike is a terrible imposition. Many grandparents are able to maintain good relationships by seeing a child for a few hours every once in a while. Maybe the grandparents could babysit for you or take your child to some of his or her sports or activities. Think creatively about this. You don't have to agree to ship your child off once a month. Find a way to make the grandparents a part of the child's life in a manner that will benefit all of you.

You may also feel that since they are the other parent's parents, your ex ought to be the one responsible for making sure the grandparents see the child. To an extent, this is true. If the other parent has a reasonable amount of visitation, there is no reason why he or she cannot make sure that the child and grandparents have time together. Discuss this with the other parent. If the other parent lives far away or fails to exercise his or her visitation, you will find that the responsibility for maintaining this relationship will fall on your shoulders.

Shared Parenting

Some families have a 50/50 arrangement in their parenting plans, in which each parent spends about half the time with the children. These kinds of arrangements can be alternate weeks, alternate months, or any other kind of schedule that nets out as an equal split. This kind of arrangement is great because it means you each get equal time with your kids, but it can be difficult because the kids are always on the move.

Shared parenting can be wonderful or it can be a complete disaster. You both get to be very involved in your children's lives on a day-to-day basis, but it can be a bit hectic and confusing at times and requires good cooperation between parents.

To make shared parenting successful, follow these suggestions.

- Be a schedule freak. Keep an accurate calendar and be clear about who is supposed to be where, and when.
- Develop a smooth transition. You're transferring your child back and forth on a regular basis, so you're going to need a solid transition plan. (See Chapter 7 for more information about transitions.)
- Accept that the other parent is going to be a regular part of your life. You're going to see a lot of each other, so it's a good idea to make some sort of peace with each other.
- Try to be flexible. Your agreement is to share your time with your children. If that means the other parent ends up with one extra day this week because of the way everyone's schedules fall, don't make a big deal out of it. Your goal should be that you end up with equal parenting times over a long period of time.

Do not count the hours and get into a detailed accounting unless there are real problems with your arrangement.

Shared Residence

Some parents work out an arrangement where, for a period of time (usually the first year or so after separation or divorce, as a transition phase), they maintain the marital residence as the children's home and each parent gets a separate apartment of their own. The parents then take turns living with the children in the marital home. For example, the mother would live at the home one week and the father would live there the next. Sometimes the parents both remain in the home and simply have separate scheduled parenting time (called nesting).

This kind of arrangement gives the children a sense of stability. They are still being parented in one home and they don't have to pack up and move around. It can be a gradual way of helping everyone adjust to the divorce. The downfalls of this are that it can be expensive (if your family is maintaining three residences instead of two), your children don't get all the changes in their life over with all at once, and you and your spouse are still sharing a living space, which can lead to conflict. To make this kind of situation work, follow these suggestions.

- Create household rules. Decide who is going to do what household chores. Not discussing these decisions is guaranteed to lead to conflict. You couldn't live together in harmony when you were married, so there is no reason to assume that you can easily do so now. Make compromises and try to come up with some rules you both can live by.
- Have financial rules in place. Decide who is paying for what and try to keep your finances as separate as possible.
- Be honest if it is not working. This kind of arrangement might work well for your family for a few months, but you might find that you or your kids are growing out of it. If that happens, reassess your situation.
- Make the kids part of your new lives. It's too confusing to have one parent just disappear for a week or however long a shift is. Make sure your child sees where you're living and understands what you're doing. Maintain regular phone, text, or Skype contact while away.

Chapter 13

Children's Ages and Stages

Your child is constantly growing and changing, so it's unrealistic to expect that a parenting plan can be set in stone throughout his or her life. The plan is going to need to change as he or she does. You can make changes simply by talking to the other parent and agreeing on them, you can meet with a mediator who will help you reach an agreement, you can speak to your attorneys and have them reach a settlement, or you can return to court and have the judge decide for you. It's always important to consider your child's current needs when making changes to your schedule.

This chapter will talk about the different needs children have, and will give you some ideas how to modify your plan as they grow. Come back to this chapter for help as your child grows or when you or your child start to feel as if the visitation plan needs some changes.

Infants

If you have an infant, your parenting plan may allow the other parent to have frequent short visits or a traditional kind of schedule where he or she has the child for weekends. Generally, short frequent visits work best for infants, so if you have a traditional plan and you find the baby is having difficulty with it, try switching to the other type of plan. Infants may display more frequent crying and problems with eating, sleeping, and digestion when they are disturbed. One complication to visitation with an infant is breastfeeding. If you are breastfeeding, then it will be difficult for the other parent to spend time greater than an hour or two alone with the child. Consider pumping and freezing some breast milk so the other parent can feed the baby from a bottle, and would thus be able to take the child to his home or relative's homes. You could also allow the father time alone with your child in your home, so you can nurse when needed.

Be aware that breastfeeding can be a very emotional issue. Don't assume that because the other parent wants to be able to spend time alone with your child that he or she is trying to interfere with breastfeeding. Explain to him or her that pediatricians do recommend that children be breastfed for at least one year and discuss the benefits of it. Suggest that he/she talk to the pediatrician to understand it better. Some women are unable to pump milk and feel it is okay for the other parent to give the baby formula when they are not available for feedings. Talk to your pediatrician or lactation consultant about this before trying it.

If you are the other parent, and the breastfeeding mother wants to try to continue breastfeeding during visitation times, you should both speak to a lactation consultant about this since it can be difficult, but not impossible.

Sleep issues are always a problem with an infant. You and the other parent should try to work together to develop a plan. Are you going to try to get the child on a schedule at night and for naps or are you going to let the child decide when sleeping happens? It's important to be consistent and work cooperatively on this. If you are trying to get the child to follow a specific schedule and the other parent doesn't do the same thing, you're going to have a cranky child. You and the other parent should work together when solid foods are introduced and need to follow a schedule for your child's meals. Follow a set schedule for introducing new foods—you want to introduce one new food at a time so that if there are any food allergies they can be easily identified and make sure you're both doing the same thing. Talk to your pediatrician for more details about this.

Parenting Together Apart: For the Residential Parent

Suggest that the other parent get some basic baby equipment to keep at his or her home so everything does not need to be transported each time. He or she can purchase a portable crib instead of a full-size one and a portable highchair seat that straps onto a chair instead of a large, free-standing highchair.

It is easy when you are the residential parent of an infant to feel as if you are doing all the hard work and the other parent is showing up for play time. Don't worry, this is only temporary. Some residential parents feel they have a hard time getting the nonresidential parent to understand the basics of baby care. Suggest that the other parent come along for well baby visits and encourage discussions with the doctor that will help bring home the points you are having a hard time getting across. Share baby care books and links with the other parent. It can be helpful to send a written schedule back and forth that you will each fill in, so you will know when the baby last ate and slept. There are also apps you can use to help track this.

SLEEP SCHEDULE CHART

Date	Time	Woke Up At	Notes

FEEDING SCHEDULE CHART

Date	Time	Amount	Notes

Toddlers

Toddlers are going through many changes and it is best to try to stick to a really tight schedule for parenting time. Don't monkey around with it if you can help it. Toddlers will experience separation anxiety and have trouble separating from whichever parent they are with. Deal with separation anxiety by taking a little more time with transitions and making them more gradual. Toddlers also start to display aggression by biting, throwing, or hitting. Deal with this by consistently saying no and removing your child from the situation or item and get the other parent on board with this as well.

When your child is a toddler, he or she may be ready to begin spending the night at the other parent's home. Usually one night a week is good way to start. You want to get him or her used to this new event and grow accustomed to sleeping at the other parent's home. You also need to personally adjust to this. This is a reality. Your child is going to spend some of his or her time alone with the other parent and will be sleeping there. It is hard to let go, but you have to help your child adjust to this. Toddlers may experience sleep disturbances, especially if they are adjusting to sleeping overnight at the other parent's home for the first time. Talk to the other parent about what works to comfort the child in the night.

Talk with the other parent about things like potty training, discipline, and sleeping schedules. Consistency really is important. Share books and links about what to expect from toddlers with the other parent.

Remember that toddlers are all about pushing the limits, and your child will want to find out what limits you and the other parent have.

Make sure the other parent has his or her home childproofed so your child cannot reach dangerous things or find small objects to put in his or her mouth. Tantrums are going to be a fact of life, and you and the other parent simply need to learn how to cope with them. A tantrum does not mean you should change your parenting plan. Tantrums are a normal part of your child's development and you both need to develop the skills needed to manage them.

Preschoolers

When your child reaches the preschool age, you'll probably find that he or she is becoming more verbal and cognitively involved. He or she will probably ask you questions that go to the very root of things, such as, "Why do you live here and Dad lives at another house?" Give brief and honest answers to these kinds of questions. A good answer is, "Because some parents don't live together."

Preschoolers can begin to handle a typical visitation schedule, such as every other weekend at the other parent's home. If you do change to this kind of schedule, do so gradually and try to make sure the other parent does continue to have some kind of weekly in-person contact with your child. This is why many nonresidential parents see their children one weeknight each week. Try to make sure your child has phone contact with the other parent on a regular basis as well.

Elementary Children

When your child begins school, you may need to make some adjustments to your schedule. It's important to make sure your child gets enough sleep on school nights. Your child can begin to spend the majority of visitation time on weekends now. Regular in-person contact during the week is important though, so consider working out a schedule where the other parent and child have dinner one weekday evening each week. Keep in contact with the other parent and your child's teacher about how things are going, and be prepared to make changes if it seems that the schedule is impacting the child's school behavior. Finding the right schedule can take some trial and error.

Your elementary age child will ask you even more probing questions about the divorce or separation and the reasons for it. Answer questions honestly, but do not give details or deeply personal information unless it truly is helpful and will not cause the child to see the other parent in a bad light. Children of this age often display their emotions about their family through physical symptoms, like headaches and stomachaches. Try to keep your child comfortable, and always see a doctor if you believe he or she is truly ill. Be supportive and loving, yet firm about the schedule.

Homework is an important consideration at this age. Elementary students now have more homework than you ever did at that age. Make sure that your child has time to get homework done at both homes and that the homework gets to school. This requires organization. Encourage your child to ask the other parent for homework help. Suggest that the other parent help out with a school project. This may mean that they will need some extra time together for trips to the library or to buy materials at a craft store to complete the project on time. Keeping the other parent involved with your child's life will directly benefit your child. Elementary children also have after-school activities and sports to consider.

Friends are becoming important at this age as well. Your child may wish to spend time with friends during visitation time. You will have to leave this decision to the other parent, but you can suggest that having a friend over will help the child feel at home at the other parent's residence and allow the other parent to get to know the child's friends.

Encourage the other parent to attend your child's sports events, concerts, and performances. These do not have to fall onto a regularly scheduled visitation day for him or her to attend as long as you are both comfortable being there at the same time, although not necessarily together.

Preteens

Kids in the eight to twelve-year age range are often called tweens since they are in a stage between early childhood and the teen years. Tweens act a lot like teens sometimes. They are interested in popular culture, fashion, music, movies, and trends, but they are still children in many ways. Just because your tween listens to the hottest new music, has her nose buried in her phone, and is sporting a new hairstyle does not mean that he or she doesn't want or need love, attention, and time from both parents.

Tweens sometimes try very hard to be perfect in the hopes that this will bring their parents back together. Make sure your child knows no one is perfect and that nothing can bring you and the other parent back together. They also often begin to take sides or assign blame for the divorce or separation (to the parents or themselves). Explain to your child that he or she is not to blame and that there are two people in a marriage or relationship, and both in some way cause a breakup.

Your child will have even more homework now, lots of friends, and activities. It's important that you continue to follow a schedule and make sure that time for both parents is built into the child's life. Let your child be active and busy, find a way for you both to be involved in his or her interests, and make sure your child continues to have time to spend together with each parent.

Teens

You remember being a teenager. Nothing about it was easy. It's even harder today, especially when you have parents who live in separate houses and who make different and sometimes competing demands on you.

Your teen deals with the divorce or separation in a way different from younger children. He or she does continue to have feelings of loss, grief, anger, and sadness, but also blames him or herself for the situation. Teens frequently feel that they will never be able to have a stable relationship and should avoid marriage. It's important to talk about these feelings with your child and help him or her understand that no blame falls on his or her shoulders, and that many marriages do work out.

Teens often feel they have had to grow up too quickly because of the divorce or separation. There isn't much you can do about this, other than to insulate him or her from disputes between you and the other parent, and avoid confiding in him or her like a friend. Teens also often worry about money, and feel involved with child support and even alimony. Don't involve your teen in child support or alimony matters. Teens do need to start to understand finances and to understand budgets, but you should not unload your financial worries on your teen. Additionally, teens feel a need to take on adult responsibility, to fill the gaps at both homes. Remember, your teen is not an adult and is not a substitute for the other parent, and should not be expected to fill his or her role.

Your teen will need to be consulted about the schedule. Independence is important at this age. Teens not only have a lot of homework and after-school activities, but friends are now the most important thing in his or her world. Many teens also have jobs. Working out a schedule may be difficult. It's going to require some compromise on all fronts. Your teen is working hard at becoming an adult, and he or she must learn that compromise is an important skill. Dating can be a conflict with visitation. What teen is going to give up time with a love interest to hang out with Mom or Dad?

You've got to somehow reach a balance. If your teen spends every weekend day and evening dating, he or she will never see the other parent and will rarely see you. Perhaps your teen can reserve maybe one weekend a month or two Sundays a month to spend with the other parent. Suggest something similar for your time together as well. Your teen needs to know that you both support his or her lifestyle, but also that you both want to spend time with him or her.

Expect to be met with resistance, outbursts, attitudes, refusals to communicate—all those things you may have done to your own parents. You will need to make changes in the schedule to accommodate your teen's life, but there does need to be some kind of regular time for the other parent. Many parents find that they are comfortable without a schedule. They let their teen drop in or stay the night at the other parent's home whenever the mood strikes. If this works for you and the other parent, then go ahead and do it. Other parents feel that they need to have a schedule to follow so they can organize their own lives. You'll have to work out what works best for your family.

If you have a plan that your teen refuses to follow no matter what you do, you need to take a look at it and determine what the problem is. Does he or she resent being away from friends? Can you make any changes or allowances that will make the plan easier to live with? Do you need to make some scheduling changes? Involve your teen in this process and demonstrate that you are willing to be flexible while still maintaining your strong commitment to your relationship.

Unfortunately, there are teens who decide they do not want to go on visitation and do not want to spend time with one of their parents. You must continue to encourage your teen to go on visitation, but when it comes right down to it, you won't be able to force him or her to go. Courts do pay attention to what teens say they want when it comes to visitation.

Talk to the other parent about the situation. Suggest that you both back off and give the teen some space. Skip some planned visits. Emphasize that the other parent should not give up and walk away. Taking some breathing room may be just what is needed, but the other parent should not throw up his or her hands and say "forget it." Your child needs the other parent to care and needs him or her to keep trying. Your teen is exercising his or her independence and you've all got to find a way to work with it.

Adult Children

Once your child is over age 18, he or she is not subject to the visitation plan any longer. This doesn't mean that your work is done: He or she still needs contact with both parents. Just because your child is technically an adult, you should not suddenly unload the truth about the other parent. Your child still needs a relationship with the other parent, and you still need to keep your mouth shut and your nose out of it. College kids and young adults still need parents.

It is hard to learn to let go and let your child become independent, and watch him or her do things that you see as mistakes. You and the other parent did the best job you could, and your child really will be fine. Pat yourself on the back for creating and raising such a good person.

Siblings

This book has talked about "your child" in a singular sense. Many parents have more than one child. When you have two or more children, you will need to cope with their conflicting schedules, conflicting abilities, and of course, with their conflicts, period.

You'll want to try to keep to a schedule that will allow your children to see the other parent at the same time when possible. They are a family unit and need to spend time all together. Things are going to come up, however. Your daughter might have a basketball game one weekend and your son might have play rehearsal another. Follow the visitation schedule and have the other parent take your kids to their planned events. The other parent can have together time and individual time with your children, just as you do.

Siblings fight. This is just a rule of the universe. Your kids don't fight because you got divorced or separated. They just fight because that's what siblings do. Set limits, create rules, and always make sure no one is physically harmed. Read some parenting books about coping with siblings and share them with the other parent. Discuss possible solutions with the other parent. Since you spend more time with your children, you probably have some strategies for managing them that you can share with the other parent. Remember that the other parent has to be allowed to work things out in his or her own way, and you cannot dictate how he or she will parent.

There will be a time when your children are certain you or the other parent are playing favorites. Often, kids have difficulty understanding that brothers or sisters of different ages need different care, supervision, and interaction. Parent as you see fit and reassure them that you both love each child equally but in a unique way.

Talking with the other parent will allow you to coordinate efforts, share insights, and work together with regard to your children.

Conclusion

Now that you've read this book, you know that there is no easy answer or quick fix to make parenting after divorce easy and comfortable for everyone. Your job as a residential parent is difficult, and the other parent has a row to hoe that's pretty tough too. You have lots of problems between the two of you that can never be worked out and lots of emotions that pop up at the most inconvenient times, but you are-and always will be—parents together. Your child is your common bond and this book was designed to help you use that to make visitation workable.

Many families get tripped up by problems with parenting plans and end up constantly going back to court. That kind of life isn't good for anyone. It's stressful not to mention expensive. This book has shown you the common pitfalls, as well as ways to work around them and avoid them completely. Now that you've read the book, share it with the other parent. Sit down together and try to follow some of the suggestions in the book. Keep this book on your bookcase and refer back to it as problems and situations come up in the future.

Making sure that your child has time and a decent relationship with the other parent may not be what you really want if you are honest with yourself, but you probably realize by now that it is what your child really and truly needs. It often feels like an imposition-you get tired of trying to accommodate the other parent and sometimes you just wish it would all go away. Hopefully, this book has given you some coping strategies to help you get through those days and tips for making things better.

If you come away with nothing else, remember that your parenting plan is not about you or the other parent, but about your child and his or her needs.

Making it work sometimes means gritting your teeth, compromising, and even sometimes just plain giving in. It will be worth it and your child will benefit from having two parents who work hard to make his or her life better.

If you have found this book helpful, there is a version of it designed specifically for the nonresidential parent (Parenting Together Apart: For the Nonresidential Parent). Suggest to the other parent that he or she read it.

Your situation will get easier as you live and work with it, and you will see your child adjust as well. The future is bright for both of you and your parenting plan is an important part of that future.

Appendix A

Sample Parenting Plans

SAMPLE 1

The following is an informal list of parenting rules developed by one couple.

- If you will be more than twenty minutes late picking up or dropping off, call or text and let the other parent know.
- Discussions about schedule changes are okay in front of the child, but arguments and heated discussions will be postponed until the child is not present.
- All of the child's laundry will be done at the residential parent's home.
- Schedule changes can be made at any time as long as we both agree. Each will notify the other parent of any changes as far in advance as possible.
- The child can call or text or Skype the parent he or she is away from at any time.
- The residential parent will share all school information that comes via hardcopy with the nonresidential parent. Each parent will sign up for email notifications on their own.

- We will attend the same parent-teacher conferences, if they can be scheduled conveniently.
- School books, instruments, and sports equipment will travel with the child.
- We will try to use each other for babysitting, if possible.
- We will try to spend some time together as a family on Christmas Day and will alternate all other holidays.
- We will respect each other's judgment about bedtimes, curfews, and daily schedules.

SAMPLE 2

The following is a formal parenting plan developed by another couple.

We agree that our son, Trevor, shall reside with his mother, Kristin, and spend time with his father, Marcus. Marcus shall have time with Trevor as follows.

Every second weekend of the month, from school dismissal on Friday until school begins on Monday morning.

Every fourth weekend of the month on Saturday from 9:00 a.m. until 8:00 p.m.

Every Wednesday from school dismissal until 7:00 p.m.

In even-numbered years on the following holidays, from 10:00 a.m. until 9:00 p.m.: New Year's Day, Memorial Day, Labor Day, Thanksgiving, Christmas Eve, and the child's birthday.

In odd-numbered years on the following holidays from 10:00 a.m. until 9:00 p.m.: Easter, Fourth of July, Columbus Day, the day after Thanksgiving, Christmas Day, New Year's Eve.

Parenting Together Apart: For the Residential Parent

Four days during winter school break and four days during spring school break, commencing at 10:00 a.m. on the first day and ending at 8:00 p.m. on the last day.

Every Father's Day and every year on Marcus's birthday.

If visitation is supposed to occur on Mother's Day or Kristin's birthday, that day in the schedule will be cancelled.

Two full weeks during summer vacation, which will not be scheduled to conflict with Kristin's family's reunion.

At other times as we both agree.
We will make the schedule together each year in January and adjust it as necessary if we both agree.

We agree that the following procedures will be followed.
Kristin shall be responsible for transporting Trevor to Marcus's home at the start of visitation, unless Marcus is scheduled to pick Trevor up at school that day.

Marcus shall be responsible for transporting Trevor to Kristin's home at the end of visitation, unless he is scheduled to return him directly to school.

Neither parent shall enter the other parent's home unless asked in.
Drop off times will have a ten-minute leeway in either direction.

Trevor will bring clothing for the time he is with Marcus, and all clothing that is taken on visitation will be returned with Trevor.
All of Trevor's belongings that are taken on visitation will return with him.

Trevor will have access to phone calls, texts, and Skype with whichever parent he is away from at the time.

Changes to the visitation schedule must be requested at least 24 hours in advance, except in emergency situations.

Neither parent will drive Trevor in the car after consuming alcohol.
Trevor will not be taken to any bars during visitation.

If either parent takes Trevor on vacation, contact information will be given to the other parent.

The following rules will apply to Trevor's routine at both homes.
Bedtime is at 9:00 p.m., unless a special event or special occasion occurs.

Both parents will make sure Trevor is dressed appropriately before leaving the house.

Screen time is not to occur until after all homework is completed, and is limited to two hours per day.

Whichever parent is with Trevor at the time is expected to transport him to soccer practice and games.

Marcus has access to Trevor's school and medical records.

Marcus is responsible for contacting the school and doctors to get copies of or access to records, report cards, notices and calendars.

Marcus will schedule a separate parent-teacher conference if he wishes to attend one.

Marcus and Kristin may attend the same school events, concerts, sports games, and ceremonies, if their schedules allow.

Appendix B

Resources

BOOKS FOR PARENTS

15 Ways to Improve Your Co-Parenting by Brette Sember

Be a Great Divorced Dad by Kenneth Condrell

The Co-Parents' Handbook: Raising Well-Adjusted, Resilient, and Resourceful Kids in a Two-Home Family from Little Ones to Young Adults By Karen Bonnell and Kristin Little

Children and Divorce: Helping Kids Cope with Separation and Divorce by Melissa Christo

Co-parenting with a Toxic Ex: What to Do When Your Ex-Spouse Tries to Turn the Kids Against You by Amy Baker and Paul Fine

Crazy Time: Surviving Divorce and Building a New Life by Abigail Trafford

The Divorce Organizer and Planner by Brette McWhorter Sember

Divorce Recovery: Proven Strategies for Divorce Recovery and Dealing with Divorce By Sarah Joy

"He Hit Me First..." When Brothers and Sisters Fight by Louise Bates Ames

No-Fight Divorce Book: Using Mediation to End Your Marriage with Less Conflict, Time, and Money by Brette McWhorter Sember

Raising A Prince Without A King: A Single Mother's Journey To Victory by LaVeda Jones

The Single Dad Detour: Directions for Fathering After Divorce By Tez Brooks

The Smart Stepfamily Marriage: Keys to Success in the Blended Family by Ron Deal and David Olson Surviving Parental Alienation: A Journey of Hope and Healing by Amy Baker and Paul Fine

Talking to Children About Divorce: A Parent's Guide to Healthy Communication at Each Stage of Divorce by Jean McBride

The Unexpected Legacy of Divorce: A 25 Year Landmark Study by Judith Wallerstein

BOOKS FOR CHILDREN
It's Not Your Fault KoKo Bear by Vicki Lansky

Dinosaurs Divorce by Marc Brown

The Divorce Help Book for Teens by Cynthia McGregor

A Smart Girl's Guide to Her Parents' Divorce by Nancy Holyoke

Parenting Together Apart: For the Residential Parent

Two Homes by Claire Masurel

What in the World Do You Do When Your Parents Divorce? by Kent Winchester

When My Parents Forgot How to Be Friends by Jennifer Moore-Mallinos

Index

Adoption, 9, 135
Adult children, 147
Anger, 11–12, 15, 18, 52
Arguments, 62, 65
Authorization to obtain medical care, 111

Bad times, dealing with, 20–21
Being present, 57
Belongings, 80–83
Birthdays, 100–101
Blame, 11–12, 59
Business transaction approach, 66–67

Changes, 9
    coping with, 102–103
Child
    age, reactions by, 18–19
    ages, 139–148
    anger, 22–23
    and anger, 11
    blame, 24–25
    changing feelings, 29
    choosing between parents, 35
    effect of divorce on, 18–19
    fear of abandonment, 25–27
    finding out what they think, 23
    focusing on, 15–16
    gender, 19
    illness, 130
    listening to, 37–38
    mental illness, 120–121
    and messages between parents, 35, 62
    promises to, 56
    reactions to divorce, 18
    relationship with other parent, 13–14
    resentment, 22–23
    and schedule, 85
    talking with about divorce, 55–56

Index

ups and downs, 19–20
wants to be with other parent, 75
your relationship with, 17–30
Child support, 66, 123–124
Civility, 59
Clothing, 62
Communication with your child, 31–38, 58
things to say, 32–34
things you should not say, 34–37
Complaints, 62
Concessions, 9
Confrontations, avoiding, 55
Co-parenting rules, 61–62
Custody, 6–8
changing, 124
shared, 136–137

Dating, 113–115
Decisions, making, 104
Denial, 18
Depression, symptoms of, 21–22, 98–99
Divided loyalties, 18, 27
Doctor. *See* Health care workers

Elementary children, 143–144
Emotions, 58
dealing with, 51–52
your changing, 27–28
Expectations, 59

Family and friends, 106–107, 112
Flexibility, 63
Food allergy, 132
Freedom, 9
Future, planning for, 12

Gender and sexuality, 127
Grandparent visitation, 135–136
Grief, 18

Index

Health care workers, 110–111
Holidays, 94–101
    and depression, 98–99
    gifts, 99–100
    realistic about, 94–95
    sharing, 99
    solving problems, 101
    traditions, 98
    traps to avoid, 98–99
    without your child, 96–97
    with your child, 95–96
Home, 59
Homeschooling, 135
Honesty, 32, 55–56
House, running alone, 103

Illness, 62, 129–130
Imprisonment, 133–134
Infants, 139–141
    charts, 141
"I" phrases, 68

Joint custody with visitation, 7

Life, having a, 104–105
Long distance parenting, 79–80
Loss, 13

Meals, 62
Medication, 83
Mental illness, 120–121
Military, 133
Mistakes, 12
Money, 35
Moving forward, 12

Nonresidential parent, 10
Nontraditional families, 8–9

Index

Other parent
    bad parenting, 122–123
    communication with, 60–69
    communication with, rules for, 68–69
    crappy parent, 78–79
    developing new relationship with, 60–61
    family and friends, 112–113
    help communicating with, 66
    new partner, 115–116
    situation, 10
    talking about, 23–24, 34–35, 53–54, 58
    time, 13–15
    times to talk, 65–66
    unbearable, 67–68
    won't use visitation, 128–129

Parental abduction, 132–133
Parenting alone, 105–106
Parenting time. *See* Custody; Visitation
Parents, importance of both, 9–10
Partner, new, 113–115
Patience, 29–30
Perfection, 52
Physical abuse, 119
Positive outlook, 12, 33
Praise, 32
Preschoolers, 143
Present, focusing on, 32–33
Preteens, 144–145
Promises, 35
Prying, 35

Reality, facing, 6–16
Reinvention, 56–57
Relocation, 131
Repetition, 68
Residence, shared, 137–138
Respect, 14, 16, 69
Responsibilities, dividing, 64–65

Index

Routine, new, 104
Rules for your child, 39–50
    bending, 48
    broken rules, 49
    changing, 49–50
    creating with other parent, 42
    creating your own, 46–47
    to discuss with other parent, 42–43
    discuss with your child, 43–46
    misinformation, 48
    other parent's rules, 46
    sample contract with teen, 45–46
    sample house rules, 44
    sample sticker chart, 45
    and sole custody, 40–41
    that are wrong, 47–48
    tips for making, 50
    yours *vs.* other parent, 41
Rules for yourself, 51–59
    being present, 57
    confrontations, avoiding, 55
    dealing with other parent, 52–53
    and emotions, 52
    making the best of it, 57–58
    parenting time, respecting, 55
    promises to your child, 56
    speaking negatively about other parent, 53–54
    talking to your child, 54–55
    timeliness, 57

Same-sex parents, 9
Schedule, 84–93, 105
    changes by child, 62
    changing, 14–15, 61–62, 88–89
    child's, 86–87
    and child's friends, 88
    conflicts, 87
    confusion, solving, 90–92
    equal time problems, 89–90

Index

    sample scheduling rules, 85–86
    saying no, 88
    talking about, 65–66
    violations, 92–93
    written, 63–64
    and your child, 85
School, 86, 108–110
Self-esteem, 18
Sexual abuse, 119
Shared custody, 7
Siblings, 147–148
Sincerity, 32
Single parent life, 102–107
Social media, 24
Sole custody with visitation, 7
Special needs child, 131
Stay at home parent, 134
Stepfamilies, 115, 117–118
Substance abuse, 120
Support, 106–107
Surrogacy, 9

Teacher. *See* School
Teens, 19, 76, 128, 145–147
    contract with, 45–46
Therapist, 21–22, 52
Timeliness, 57, 62
Time with your child, 16
Toddlers, 142
Transitions, 76–77
Transportation, 62, 85
Travel for work, 133
Trust, 18

Vacation, 62, 80
Violation of court order, 122
Visitation, 6–8
    encouraging and assisting with, 70–83
    ending, 125–126

Index

feelings about, 71
kids don't want to go, 73–75
parenting who won't use, 128–129
responsibility for, 72–73
superceding, 129–130
supervised, 126–127
talking about with your child, 71–72

Weather, 129

About the Author

Brette Sember is a retired divorce and family attorney and family mediator. She focused her practice on representing children in divorce and custody cases. She was on the Law Guardian panel in three different New York state counties. As part of this role, she visited child clients in their homes, visited their schools, saw them interact with both parents, and facilitated and attended therapy sessions with them when needed. She worked closely with parents, teachers, social workers, and therapists, as well as attorneys for both sides.

She is the author of more than 40 books including *The Complete Divorce Guide, Rebuild Your Financial Life After Divorce, How to Avoid Returning to Family Court*, and *15 Ways to Improve Your Co-Parenting*.

Her website is www.BretteSember.com.

www.ingramcontent.com/pod-product-compliance
Lightning Source LLC
Chambersburg PA
CBHW020422010526
44118CB00010B/383